PRAXIS® 5712 CORE Reading

Core Academic Skills for Educators: Reading

By: Preparing Teachers In America™

This page is intentionally left blank.

PRAXIS® is a registered trademark of the Educational Testing Services. Any reference to PRAXIS® is not intended to imply an affiliation with, or sponsorship by Educational Testing Services, or any other entity authorized to provide official PRAXIS® assessment services.

© 2017 by Preparing Teachers In America

Publication by Preparing Teachers In America Publication Services, a division of Preparing Teachers In America

All rights reserved. The text of this publication, or any part thereof, may not be reproduced in any manner whatsoever without the written permission from Preparing Teachers In America. Any violation of copyright laws will be subject to possible criminal charges and/or civil penalties.

Printed in the United States of America

ISBN-13: 978-1542311663

ISBN-10: 1542311667

The author and the publisher make no warranties with respect to the correctness or completeness of the content contain in this publication and specifically disclaim all warranties whatsoever. Advice, strategies, and suggestions described may not be suitable for every case. Providing web addresses or other (information) services in this publication does not mean/imply that the author or publisher endorses information or websites. Neither the author nor publisher shall be liable for damages arising herefrom. Websites may be infected by computer viruses. The author and publisher shall not be held responsible for any damage resulted herefrom. Websites (content) may have altered since the time the author described them in this booklet and this booklet is read. There are no guarantees attached to the publication. The content of this publication is best practices, suggestions, common mistakes, and interpretation, and the author and the publisher are not responsible for any information contained in the publication.

Any services provided by the publication, authors, or company are with the understanding that services can be terminated with or without notice. In rendering services, the author and the publisher are not responsible for any information communicated. Users agree not to hold the service (author/publisher/company) or its employees liable for any services (information) provided or any information displayed on the website. Users release the service from any claims or any kind of damage. The author, publisher, services, and/or company are not responsible for any accuracy or legitimacy of the information provided during rendering services. There are no guarantees attached to services.

No institutions (public or private) have permission to reproduce (in any form) the contents of this publication.

This page is intentionally left blank.

Free Online Email Tutoring Services

All preparation guides purchased directly from Preparing Teachers In America includes a free three month email tutoring subscription. Any resale of preparation guides does not qualify for a free email tutoring subscription.

What is Email Tutoring?

Email Tutoring allows buyers to send questions to tutors via email. Buyers can send any questions regarding the exam processes, strategies, content questions, or practice questions.

Preparing Teachers In America reserves the right not to answer questions with or without reason(s).

How to use Email Tutoring?

Buyers need to send an email to onlinepreparationservices@gmail.com requesting email tutoring services. Buyers may be required to confirm the email address used to purchase the preparation guide or additional information prior to using email tutoring. Once email tutoring subscription is confirmed, buyers will be provided an email address to send questions to. The three month period will start the day the subscription is confirmed.

Any misuse of email tutoring services will result in termination of service. Preparing Teachers In America reserves the right to terminate email tutoring subscription at anytime with or without notice.

Comments and Suggestions

All comments and suggestions for improvements for the study guide and email tutoring services need to be sent to onlinepreparationservices@gmail.com.

This page is intentionally left blank.

Table of Content

About the Exam and Study Guide 1

Exam Answer Sheet Test 1 5

Reading Practice Exam 1 – Questions 7

Exam Key – Practice Exam 1 41

Reading Practice Exam 1 – Questions and Explanations 43

Exam Answer Sheet Test 2 85

Reading Practice Exam 2 – Questions 87

Exam Key – Practice Exam 2 121

Reading Practice Exam 2 – Questions and Explanations 123

This page is intentionally left blank.

About the Exam and Study Guide

What is the PRAXIS® CORE Reading Exam?

The PRAXIS® CORE Reading is an exam to test potential teachers' competencies in basic reading skills necessary to pursue a teaching career. The exam is aligned with the Common Core State Standards, and the exam covers the following content areas:

- Key Ideas and Details
- Craft, Structure, and Language Skills
- Integration of Knowledge and Ideas

The exam is timed at 85 minutes and consists of 56 questions. The 56 selected-response questions are based on knowledge obtained in a bachelor's degree program. The questions are based on reading passages and statements. The exam contains some questions that may not count toward the score.

What topics are covered on the exam?

The following are some topics covered on the exam:

- drawing inferences
- identifying summaries
- identifying main ideas and purposes
- determining tone and attitude
- identifying organization of passages
- distinguishing between fact and opinion
- understanding figurative language
- identifying relationships among sentences
- drawing conclusions
- determining assumptions

What is included in this study guide book?

This guide includes two full length practice exams for the PRAXIS® CORE Reading Exam along with detail explanations. The recommendation is to take the exams under exam conditions and a quiet environment.

This page is intentionally left blank.

Practice Test 1

This page is intentionally left blank.

Exam Answer Sheet Test 1

Below is an optional answer sheet to use to document answers.

Question Number	Selected Answer	Question Number	Selected Answer
1		29	
2		30	
3		31	
4		32	
5		33	
6		34	
7		35	
8		36	
9		37	
10		38	
11		39	
12		40	
13		41	
14		42	
15		43	
16		44	
17		45	
18		46	
19		47	
20		48	
21		49	
22		50	
23		51	
24		52	
25		53	
26		54	
27		55	
28		56	

This page is intentionally left blank.

Reading Practice Exam 1 – Questions

Written by Simon J. Barrington

When charged with a crime, one option is to plea out the charge. A plea bargain is an arrangement between a defendant and a prosecutor, in which the defendant agrees to plead guilty or no contest. Most lawyers push clients toward a plea bargain, so they do not have to spend a lot of time on the case.

QUESTION 1

Which of the following is an unstated assumption made in the statement?

A. plea bargains are the best options to a speedy conclusion
B. lawyers make easy money by pushing plea bargains
C. defendants have to agree to the plea bargains
D. plea bargains are very common
E. plea bargains are easy to get

Answer:

Written by Elizabeth Cady Stanton

I urge a sixteenth amendment, because "manhood suffrage," or a man's government, is civil, religious, and social disorganization. The male element is a destructive force, stern, selfish, aggrandizing, loving war, violence, conquest, acquisition, breeding in the material and moral world alike discord, disorder, disease, and death. See what a record of blood and cruelty the pages of history reveal! Through what slavery, slaughter, and sacrifice, through what inquisitions and imprisonments, pains and persecutions, black codes and gloomy creeds, the soul of humanity has struggled for the centuries, while mercy has veiled her face and all hearts have been dead alike to love and hope!

QUESTION 2

The passage uses words that start with the same letters (ex. material and moral, discord, disorder, disease, and death, slavery, slaughter, and sacrifice, inquisitions and imprisonments, and pains and persecutions). What is the purpose of doing so?

- A. it is common practice
- B. shows exaggerations
- C. grabs the readers' attention
- D. shows the importance of the topic
- E. shows the need for the amendment

Answer:

QUESTION 3

Which of the following best describes the tone of the passage?

- A. regret
- B. negative
- C. appealing
- D. incepting
- E. intolerable

Answer:

QUESTION 4

What is the purpose of the paragraph?

A. to explain the horrors of society
B. to convey that despite horror in society there is hope
C. to get an amendment ratified
D. manhood suffrage is the cause of problems
E. people have died for love and hope

Answer:

Written by Anonymous Author

In America, majority of children attend elementary and secondary public institutions in which they spend approximately seven hours, on average, of their day in school. During school, children eat two meals along with snacks. Having vending machines selling unhealthy snacks, such as sodas and processed snack foods, have prompted some debate. Unhealthy foods are major cause of obesity, diabetes, and heart disease, and school institutions promote the idea of good health, so to place vending machines in school corridors is hypocritical of school leaders. Vending machines with unhealthy options should not be allowed on school properties.

With students spending more time in school than with their parents, schools have a responsibility to convey an incontrovertible message regarding good eating habits. Schools are a very influential force in developing young people's minds. Most schools require health education, in which students are conveyed the message of the benefits of fruits and vegetables, fiber, and protein…Schools are an institution with authority, similar to parents. If a father constantly gave his son a lunch of Lay's chips and a Coca Cola, he would be considered a bad father, especially if the child suffered health complications. Institutions that are allowed to have unhealthy options in vending machines are similarly negligent…

Giving students the option to use healthy vending machines supports the growing problems associated with junk food, such as obesity, diabetes, heart disease, and laziness…Individuals who are obese might not feel very happy with their appearance. This is especially true when looking at the number of surgical options individuals undertake to reduce the weight on their body. In addition, treating heart disease, stroke, and diabetes is expensive. In order to effectively initiate solving the problem, schools have to be involved in establishing the idea of good eating habits at a young age. Providing healthier options in public schools will not only reduce obesity among children, but it will also give the children energy they need. Teachers often encounter students' laziness, tiredness, and sleepiness especially in the afternoon due to heavy food intake. Offering healthier food options will give the students the energy they need to go through the afternoon sessions. The negative impact of processed foods and sodas is significant, and schools don't need to have vending machines to be enablers of the problem associated with unhealthy eating.

The students of our public schools are the future of our society, so schools need to ensure individuals have healthy options to eat to reduce the chances of obesity, diabetes, and heart disease. Vending machines selling junk food have no place where students go to be educated.

QUESTION 5

Which of the following most weaken the argument of the passage?

A. Parents are more responsible of what students eat.
B. Students should have the right to choose what to eat.
C. Some individuals have medical problems that require them to eat sugary snacks.
D. Students who want unhealthy snacks can find it outside of school.
E. Discussing eating healthy options in health education classes covers school responsibilities.

Answer:

QUESTION 6

Which of the following is the strongest statement from the passage that supports the idea of banning unhealthy vending machines?

A. Schools have a responsibility not only to teach students the importance of eating healthy but also to practice that message.
B. Giving students the option to use healthy vending machines supports the growing problems associated with junk food, such as obesity, diabetes, heart disease, and laziness.
C. With students spending more time in school than with their parents, schools have a responsibility to convey an incontrovertible message regarding good eating habits.
D. Vending machines selling junk food have no place where students go to be educated.
E. When schools are allowed to have vending machines that sell sodas and snack foods, the message of eating healthy is contradicted.

Answer:

QUESTION 7

Which of the following best explains the relationship between the following two sentences?

Sentence 1: Schools are an institution with authority, similar to parents.

Sentence 2: If a father constantly gave his son a lunch of Lay's chips and a Coca Cola, he would be considered a bad father, especially if the child suffered health complications.

   A. Sentence 2 is an example that relates to the statement in Sentence 1.
   B. Sentence 2 provides validation to Sentence 1.
   C. Sentence 2 strengthens the statement in Sentence 1.
   D. Sentence 2 is similar to Sentence 1.
   E. Sentence 2 expands on the idea of Sentence 1.

Answer:

QUESTION 8

Which of the following negative consequences is not directly mentioned regarding junk food?

   A. tiredness
   B. heart disease
   C. bad grades
   D. sleepiness
   E. laziness

Answer:

QUESTION 9

Which of the following best describes the purpose of the first passage?

A. Inform readers that vending machines with junk food is a problem in public institutions.
B. Take a firm stand against having vending machines on school properties.
C. Inform readers that healthy food options are absolutely necessary.
D. Discuss the time students spend in school.
E. Communicate the different aspects of junk foods.

Answer:

QUESTION 10

From the passage, it can be inferred that healthy foods will

A. eliminate diabetes and heart diseases.
B. help promote a better image for schools.
C. give more options for students during lunch.
D. help students in the classroom.
E. eliminate obesity in schools across the nation.

Inferred: deduce or conclude (information) from evidence and reasoning rather than from explicit statement.

Answer:

QUESTION 11

Which of the following is the most appropriate replacement word for enablers?

- A. blowers
- B. captures
- C. detractor
- D. promoters
- E. supporters

Answer:

QUESTION 12

Which of the following best explains the relationship between the two sentences?

Sentence 1: Vending machines with unhealthy options should not be allowed on school properties.

Sentence 2: Vending machines selling junk food have no place where students go to be educated.

- A. Sentence 1 is a thesis statement and Sentence 2 is a repetitive form of Sentence 1.
- B. Sentence 2 is an example that relates to the statement in Sentence 1.
- C. Sentence 2 strengthens the statement in Sentence 1.
- D. Sentence 2 provides validation to Sentence 1.
- E. Sentence 2 expands on the idea of Sentence 1.

Answer:

QUESTION 13

Which of the following can be added to the passage to strengthen the position?

- A. Obesity, diabetes, and heart diseases have caused countless lives in America.
- B. Schools have greater responsibilities than parents as students spend more time in school.
- C. Junk food has many harmful ingredients that are hurtful to children.
- D. All doctors recommend having healthy options in school to eat.
- E. None of the above

Answer:

QUESTION 14

What is the meaning of incontrovertible?

- A. questionable
- B. incontestable
- C. correct
- D. acceptable
- E. arguable

Answer:

Source One

Written by Asa Gace Benetton

In recent years, Indiana has seen a sharp decline in new teachers entering into the classroom. Between 2008 and 2015, Indiana has seen about a 30 percent decline in the number of first-time teacher licenses being given by the Indiana Department of Education. In fact, comparing data from 2014 and 2015, the number of licenses issued to first-time teachers was down 21 percent. The lack of interest in becoming a teacher is the result of a decade long decline in enrollment in education programs in some major universities in Indiana. The shortage of teachers in Indiana has become so significant that is has been raised to the state legislature. Public officials are proposing solutions such as discussing more about the teaching profession with young adults, creating more education classes, and seeking out teachers of diverse background…

Others indicate that the new teacher certification examinations are the cause of teachers being swayed from perusing teaching careers. Some potential teachers have taken the exam multiple times and have changed career paths due to having difficulty passing the certification exams. Many also blame the implementation of the Common Core State Standards in 2014, which made it harder to deliver quality education. As a result, the teaching profession has obtained a negative perception. Only time will tell if the proposed solution will solve the problem of teacher shortage in Indiana.

Source Two

Written by Leonard Jacob Farmington

Most States across the nation are seeing shortages in teachers, including California. For the last couple of years, California has seen a major decline in issuing teaching certifications, and districts are forced to scramble to fill those positions. California is the most populated State in the United States, but is one of the States with the least amount of certified teachers. For example, California ranks the lowest with high student-to-teacher ratios; the State would need 100,000 additional teachers right now to bring that ratio down to the national average. Moreover, according to the Center for the Future of Teaching and Learning, California will need about an additional 100,000 teachers over the next decade…

Experts claim that recruitment of teachers in the State has declined to the lowest in history, and efforts made to retain qualified teachers have declined. The salaries of teachers are a lot less than salaries of other professions that require comparable education, training, and skills. With the rising cost of living, it is harder for individuals to initiate or continue pursuing a teaching career.

QUESTION 15

Passage 1 indicates creating more education classes as one solution

    A. to get students informed about education.
    B. to help potential teachers in gaining best practices.
    C. to help potential teachers on new teacher certification exams.
    D. to get students more interested in education.
    E. to give more opportunities to get teaching degree.

Answer:

QUESTION 16

Which of the following best describes the relationship between Sentence 1 and 2?

Sentence 1: Between 2008 and 2015, Indiana has seen about a 30 percent decline in the number of first-time teacher licenses being given by the Indiana Department of Education.

Sentence 2: The lack of interest in becoming a teacher is the result of a decade long decline in enrollment in education programs in some major universities in Indiana.

    A. Sentence 2 provides a possible reason supporting Sentence 1.
    B. Sentence 2 contradicts Sentence 1.
    C. Sentence 1 provides counterargument for Sentence 2.
    D. Sentence 1 gives an example of problem mentioned in Sentence 2.
    E. Sentence 2 provides data for Sentence 1.

Answer:

QUESTION 17

It can be inferred that teaching certification exams are harder because

- A. of updated standards.
- B. of lack of good education program.
- C. of the Common Core State Standards.
- D. of the lack of interest.
- E. of the shortage of teachers

Answer:

QUESTION 18

Which of the following statements can weaken Passage 1 position?

- A. The shortage of teachers will eventually be solved.
- B. Some individuals have a positive perception for the teaching profession.
- C. In 2014 and 2015, more individuals changed their careers to be teachers.
- D. Changes in teacher certification exams are the main reasons for shortage of changes.
- E. Common Core State Standards did help some schools in the United States in improving math skills.

Answer:

QUESTION 19

According to Passage 2, which of the following is not a reason for teacher shortage?

  A. recruitment
  B. salaries
  C. training
  D. cost of living
  E. retention

Answer:

QUESTION 20

Which of the following is an acceptable replacement for the word comparable?

  A. similar
  B. equivalent
  C. identical
  D. the same level
  E. duplicate

Answer:

QUESTION 21

Which of the following is a common reason for teacher shortage in both passages?

  A. salaries
  B. training
  C. retention
  D. living cost
  E. recruitment

Answer:

QUESTION 22

Both passages present all the following except?

- A. numerical data
- B. possible solutions
- C. reasons for the problem
- D. public officials finding solutions
- E. example of problems faced in States

Answer:

QUESTION 23

Passage 2 presents a weaker position than Passage 1 for teacher shortage because

- A. California has a larger population, so teacher shortage issue is something that is more likely.
- B. California does not have public officials involved in implementing solutions.
- C. California needs a lot more teachers over the next decade.
- D. the cost of living is contributing to teacher shortage.
- E. districts are forced to scramble to fill those positions.

Answer:

QUESTION 24

Based on both passages, it can be inferred that

- A. the problem of teacher shortage is being addressed in both States.
- B. recruitment is the key to solving the problem of teacher shortage.
- C. the problem of teacher shortage will never be solved.
- D. the problem of teacher shortage has always been in existence.
- E. the problem of teacher shortage is the most critical issue in both Indiana and California.

Answer:

QUESTION 25

Which of the following sentence from Passage 1 can best be placed at the end of the second paragraph of Passage 2?

A. As a result, the teaching profession has obtained a negative perception.
B. Many also blame the implementation of the Common Core State Standards in 2014, which made it harder to deliver quality education.
C. Others indicate that the new teacher certification examinations are the cause of teachers being swayed from perusing teaching careers.
D. In fact, comparing data from 2014 and 2015, the number of licenses issued to first-time teachers was down 21 percent.
E. Public officials are proposing solutions such as discussing more about the teaching profession with young adults, creating more education classes, and seeking out teachers of diverse background.

Answer:

Written by Lord Chesterfield

THERE is no branch of a man's education, no portion of his intercourse with other men, and no quality which will stand him in good stead more frequently than the capability of writing a good letter upon any and every subject. In business, in his intercourse with society, in, I may say, almost every circumstance of his life, he will find his pen called into requisition. Yet, although so important, so almost indispensable an accomplishment, it is one which is but little cultivated, and a letter, perfect in every part, is a great rarity.

In the composition of a good letter there are many points to be considered, and we take first the simplest and lowest, namely, the spelling.

Many spell badly from ignorance, but more from carelessness. The latter, writing rapidly, make, very often, mistakes that would disgrace a schoolboy. If you are in doubt about a word, do not from a feeling of false shame let the spelling stand in its doubtful position hoping that, if wrong, it will pass unnoticed, but get a dictionary, and see what is the correct orthography. Besides the actual misplacing of letters in a word there is another fault of careless, rapid writing, frequently seen. This is to write two words in one, running them together. I have more than once seen with him written withim, and for her stand thus, forer. Strange, too, as it may seem, it is more frequently the short, common words that are misspelled than long ones. They flow from the pen mechanically, while over an unaccustomed word the writer unconsciously stops to consider the orthography. Chesterfield, in his advice to his son, says:

"I come now to another part of your letter, which is the orthography, if I may call bad spelling orthography. You spell induce, enduce; and grandeur, you spell grandure; two faults of which few of my housemaids would have been guilty. I must tell you that orthography, in the true sense of the word, is so absolutely necessary for a man of letters, or a gentleman, that one false spelling may fix ridicule upon him for the rest of his life; and I know a man of quality, who never recovered the ridicule of having spelled wholesome without the w.

QUESTION 26

What is the main idea expressed in the passage?

    A. using the right orthography is important in writing
    B. it is important to write a good letter
    C. correct spelling of the English language is vital
    D. it is important to watch out for careless mistakes
    E. writing is important for obtaining good education

Answer:

QUESTION 27

What is the purpose of the passage?

    A. watch out for careless mistakes
    B. know how to write a letter
    C. explain the process of writing a letter
    D. convey the reader that spelling is important
    E. let his son know that orthography is important

Answer:

QUESTION 28

Which of the following best describes the organization pattern of the passage?

    A. importance
    B. process
    C. chronological
    D. topical
    E. problem-solution

Answer:

23

QUESTION 29

This passage shows bias in favor of:

A. writing letters
B. traditional spelling of the English language
C. using correct wording
D. non-educated writers
E. using dictionary

Answer:

QUESTION 30

What is the tone of this passage?

A. negative
B. positive
C. conservative
D. earnest
E. honest

Answer:

QUESTION 31

Which of the following can be inferred from the passage?

A. disagreement exists over whether traditional or phonetic spelling is preferable
B. spelling errors can happen on common words used regularly
C. a good letter must be error free of spelling mistakes
D. the writer is trying to make the letter personal to his son
E. using the right orthography is critical for good spelling

Answer:

QUESTION 32

Enrollment of Students at Bunker Hill University - 2005

	Males	Females	Total
College of Business	250	300	550
College of Engineering	162	85	247
College of Liberal Arts	144	225	369
College of Natural Sciences	325	336	661
College of Technology	114	96	210

The table above shows enrollment of students in different college departments at the Bunker Hill University in 2005. Which conclusion about enrollment at the Bunker Hill University is best supported by the table?

A. The College of Natural Sciences had the most number of enrollments in 2015.
B. Bunker Hill University is not seeing decline in enrollment.
C. Bunker Hill University has satisfied enrollment requirements for 2005.
D. The College of Natural Sciences has greater chance of having more male enrollment than female in the future.
E. The College of Engineering has greater chance of having more female enrollment than male in the future.

Answer:

Written by Anonymous Author

In America, education has long been considered a priceless and enduring asset. However, when this benefit is deliberately being denied, actions must be undertaken to defend his or her educational rights. History does indeed portray this idea, particularly the case of Brown v. Board of Education of Topeka, Kansas. This class action lawsuit is believed to be one of the most important decisions of the Supreme Court. Basically, the case was a milestone in the innovation of outlawing segregation in public schools because segregation violated the Equal Protection Clause of the Fourteenth Amendment. The decision of the courts intensified the hope and faith of many African Americans. The decision was a key to encouraging more people to take a stand for their rights. To this day, the Supreme Court ruling undoubtedly has an immeasurable impact on the lives of countless African Americans. Today, African Americans can attend any public school and sit across from whites, without any racial discrimination.

QUESTION 33

From the passage, which of the following can be interpreted as not completely accurate?

- A. Education is considered an enduring asset.
- B. Brown v. Board of Education of Topeka, Kansas had a huge impact in America.
- C. Equal Protection Clause of the Fourteenth Amendment supported the decision made by the Supreme Court.
- D. African Americans can attend any public school without any racial discrimination.
- E. Taking a stand can results in a change.

Answer:

QUESTION 34

What is a better replacement word for innovation?

A. notion
B. creation
C. efforts
D. plight
E. improvement

Answer:

QUESTION 35

What is the relationship between these two sentences?

Sentence 1: In America, education has long been considered a priceless and enduring asset.

Sentence 2: To this day, the Supreme Court ruling undoubtedly has an immeasurable impact on the lives of countless African Americans.

A. Sentence 2 analyzes the comment in sentence 1.
B. Sentence 1 provides support to the information in sentence 2.
C. Sentence 2 explains the main idea of sentence 1.
D. Sentence 1 defines education and sentence 2 provides an impact.
E. Sentence 2 counters the main idea of sentence 1.

Answer:

Written by Anonymous Author

In my opinion, much of the real estate troubles have come from the sub-prime market, meaning buyers were getting in over their heads. Either they did not put down sufficient down payments or their debt ratios were out of line. What may have happened is that banks and mortgage companies were seeking continued growth and began creating additional programs for this sub-prime market, such as interest -- only and other more aggressive programs -- many with adjustable rates. This created a larger pool of people who were able to afford homes. However, many of these buyers have marginal credit worthiness and have now begun to fall behind on mortgage payments, taxes, and credit card payments, which fueled the foreclosure crisis.

As anyone in the real estate business knows, the housing market is cyclical: as interest rates drop, the housing market picks up, and as interest rates rise, the apartment rental market picks up. The commercial market, which includes apartment complexes, should begin to see a decrease in vacancy and an increase in rental income in the apartment sector. People need a place to live and most people facing foreclosure will need to rent houses or apartments. As for the outlook for next year, I think the meltdown is not as dire as the media reports. People still need a place to live, thus, as long as unemployment stays low in most areas, next year should probably see real estate prices decline slightly. Housing prices will level off and drop in some of the condo markets such as Florida, Arizona, Vegas and parts of the Carolinas. As for the rest of the country, I foresee a cooling period with modest gains in value over the next couple of years. But, then again, who knows for certain what will happen?

The increase in foreclosure properties does benefit consumers and will probably impact the real estate market positively. I believe that with the rise in foreclosures, middle class families will take advantage of foreclosure properties because they cost much less. Even though foreclosed homes need some repairs, the benefits outweigh the costs. When my family purchased a foreclosed house, we repaired the damages ourselves. We painted all the walls, replaced tiles, and repaired other minor damage, and it only cost $1,000, as opposed to hiring a contractor, which would have cost $6,000.

Education and immigration can significantly impact the housing market. With more people obtaining higher education, income will substantially increase, making buying a house a much easier task. According to the "Housing Opportunities in Foreign-Born Market," since 1995 immigrants contribute to one-third of the household growth in the United States. Immigrants, who become U.S. citizens, own homes at substantially higher rates than non-citizens across all age groups. Looking at the history of immigrants in reference to real estate and today's increase in immigration rates, leads me to believe that perhaps investments in residential properties will increase.

People will always possess the desire to own a home. A lovely family, a good job, and a wonderful house portray the American dream. In my opinion, since many people strive to make their dream a reality, the housing market will certainly not suffer a severe blow over the next year or even in the long run.

QUESTION 36

The tone of this passage could best be described as

A. optimistic
B. harsh
C. critical
D. cunning
E. helpful

Answer:

QUESTION 37

One can infer that the housing market is

A. not going to survive one day.
B. going to survive harsh times.
C. going to require many architects.
D. going to be lucrative due to condos.
E. always going to be a sub-prime market.

Answer:

QUESTION 38

   I. sub-prime market
   II. low down payment
   III. insufficient debt ratios
   IV. immigration

Of the above, which of the following contributed to the foreclosure crisis?

   A. I and II
   B. I and III
   C. I, II, and IV
   D. I, II, and III
   E. I, II, III, and IV

Answer:

QUESTION 39

Which of the following best describes what the passage is conveying?

   A. The passage is conveying the reasons for the foreclosure crisis, condition of the current market, and future outlook of the housing market.
   B. The passage is conveying the factors that contribute to the strength of the housing market.
   C. The passage is conveying the importance of the housing market and understanding the foreclosure crisis.
   D. The passage is conveying the different reasons for the foreclosure crisis.
   E. The passage is conveying the future outlook of the housing market.

Answer:

QUESTION 40

Which of the following is best to evaluate the validity of the author's claim regarding Florida, Arizona, Vegas and parts of the Carolinas?

A. Provide an example of housing prices leveling off in another State.
B. Provide an example of housing prices leveling off and dropping in the condo markets from 10 years ago.
C. Provide explanation of possible future leveling off and dropping in the condo markets.
D. Provide example of data or study from at least one State showing the possible leveling off and dropping in the condo markets.
E. Provide details of which cities exactly will level off and drop in condo markets.

Answer:

QUESTION 41

According to the passage, who benefits the most when there is a foreclosure crisis?

A. banks
B. investors
C. middle class families
D. immigrants
E. low-income families

Answer:

QUESTION 42

What is the purpose of using personal experience in paragraph 5?

A. to strengthen the argument
B. to establish a personal connection
C. to give an example of how foreclosure property can be financially beneficial
D. to explain how foreclosure property can be repaired
E. to explain the importance of getting a foreclosure property

Answer:

QUESTION 43

What is the relationship between Sentence 1 and Sentence 2?

Sentence 1: Looking at the history of immigrants in reference to real estate and today's increase in immigration rates, leads me to believe that perhaps investments in residential properties will increase.

Sentence 2: In my opinion, since many people strive to make their dream a reality, the housing market will certainly not suffer a severe blow over the next year or even in the long run.

A. Sentence 1 supports the statement in Sentence 2.
B. Sentence 1 explains the statement in Sentence 2.
C. Sentence 1 weakens the statement in Sentence 2.
D. Sentence 1 expands the statement in Sentence 2.
E. Sentence 1 and Sentence 2 do not have a relationship.

Answer:

QUESTION 44

What is the purpose of the following statement: "But, then again, who knows for certain what will happen?"

- A. housing market is gaining strength
- B. the author's confidence is low
- C. there are many interpretation for the housing market
- D. housing market is a very fickle area
- E. housing market has a path forward

Answer:

QUESTION 45

What is the purpose of the sixth paragraph?

- A. to give reason for why the housing market can be cyclical
- B. to give information on factors that impact the housing market
- C. to provide data related to the housing market
- D. to strength the argument that the housing market can survive in the long run
- E. to convey immigrants can contribute to the housing market

Answer:

QUESTION 46

What is a common solution mentioned in the passage when individuals are faced with foreclosure?

- A. selling their homes
- B. renting a property
- C. refinancing existing loan
- D. getting a condo
- E. getting another loan

Answer:

Written by Benjamin Banneker to Thomas Jefferson, framer of the Declaration of Independence

Sir, suffer me to recall to your mind that time in which the arms and tyranny of the British Crown were exerted with every powerful effort in order to reduce you to a State of Servitude, look back I entreat you on the variety of dangers to which you were exposed; reflect on that time in which every human aid appeared unavailable, and in which even hope and fortitude wore the aspect of inability to the conflict…

This sir, was a time in which you clearly saw into the injustice of a state of slavery and in which you had just apprehensions of the horrors of its condition, it was now, sir, that your abhorrence thereof was so excited, that you publickly held forth this true and valuable doctrine, which is worthy to be recorded and remembered in all succeeding ages. "We hold these truths to be self-evident, that all men are created equal, and that they are endowed by their creator with certain unalienable rights, that among these are life, liberty and the pursuit of happiness." [Declaration of Independence]

Here, sir, was a time in which your tender feelings for yourselves had engaged you thus to declare, you were then impressed with proper ideas of the great valuation of liberty and the free possession of those blessings to which you were entitled by nature…you should at the same time counteract his mercies in detaining by fraud and violence so numerous a part of my brethren under groaning captivity and cruel oppression, that you should at the same time be found guilty of that most criminal act which you professedly detested in others with respect to yourselves.

earnest

#	Ans	✓	#	Ans	✓	#	Ans	✓
1	A	✓	27	E D		53	C	✓
2	C	✓	28	B	✓	54	D	✓
3	C	E	29	D B		55	B	✓
4	C	✓	30	C D		56	D	✓
5	D	✓	31	E A		57		
6	D	B	32	D	✓	58		
7	A	✓	33	D	✓	59		
8	C	✓	34	C	✓	60		
9	B	✓	35	B	✓			
10	A, D ✗		36	A	✓			
11	D	✓	37	B	✓			
12	B	A	38	C, B D				
13	D	A	39	A	✓			
14	B	✓	40	A D				
15	D	✓	41	C	✓			
16	A	✓	42	B C				
17	C	✓	43	A	✓			
18	C	✓	44	D	✓			
19	A E		45	D	✓			
20	✗, D		46	B	✓			
21	E	✓	47	B E				
22	D	✓	48	B	✓			
23	B	A	49	C				
24	E	A	50	C				
25	E	A	51	C				
26	C	✓	52	C				

QUESTION 47

I. he does not want to antagonize Jefferson
II. reason with Jefferson
III. has utmost respect for Jefferson
IV. destroys the possible notion that race makes people inferior

Of the above, why does Banneker use the word "Sir" multiple times?

A. I and II
B. I and III
C. I, II, and III
D. I, II, and IV
E. I, II, III, and IV

Answer:

QUESTION 48

What is the purpose of the letter?

A. communicate the horror of slavery
B. argue against slavery
C. argue against tyranny
D. bring about change to society
E. bring about kindness to the world

Answer:

QUESTION 49

What is the strength of using the quote "We hold these truths to be self-evident, that all men are created equal, and that they are endowed by their creator with certain unalienable rights, that among these are life, liberty and the pursuit of happiness."?

    A. the quote is indicating that all men are equal
    B. the quote is important in American history
    C. the quote is written by Jefferson himself
    D. the quote indicates individuals should be happy
    E. the quote is good example of how life should be in America

Answer:

QUESTION 50

What is the tone of the second paragraph?

    A. neutral
    B. bias
    C. dark
    D. disinterested
    E. pale

Answer:

QUESTION 51

Which of the following quotes from the letter might Jefferson disagree or dislike the most?

A. "Sir, suffer me to recall to your mind that time in which the arms and tyranny of the British Crown were exerted with every powerful effort in order to reduce you to a State of Servitude…"
B. "…the present freedom and tranquility which you enjoy you have mercifully received and that it is the peculiar blessing of Heaven."
C. "…that you should at the same time be found guilty of that most criminal act which you professedly detested in others with respect to yourselves."
D. "…how pitiable is it to reflect that although you were so fully convinced of the benevolence of the Father of mankind…"
E. "…Job proposed to his friends, "put your souls in their souls stead," thus shall your hearts be enlarged with kindness and benevolence towards them…"

Answer:

QUESTION 52

Benjamin Banneker describes slavery as all the following except:

A. injustice
B. horror
C. danger
D. cruel
E. criminal

Answer:

Written by Anonymous Author

The American dream that many strive to reach is to own a home. Finding a home can be a very challenging endeavor as it takes some individuals' months to even years to get a home. From deciding location to square feet to interior designs to cost, families have to weigh the various options and make some trades to be able to settle on a dream home. Otherwise, the duration of finding a home can be very lengthy to at times even impossible. In fact, the process can be lengthy to the point where it becomes discouraging for some. For most families, buying a home will be done once in their life times, so ensuring that most needs are in the home are critical. Some families who are unable to find existing homes to suit their needs and are wealthy seek options of building a custom home. Custom homes are completely tailored to individual family needs. Going the route of a custom home can be a lengthy and expensive approach; however, some families go this route to reach the American dream. Home buying is not a simple process, but certainly a rewarding process.

QUESTION 53

What is the main idea of the passage?

    A. Home buying is a rewarding process.
    B. Many options exist when it comes to home buying.
    C. Home buying can be a challenging endeavor.
    D. Home buying requires trade off.
    E. Home buying is the American dream.

Answer:

QUESTION 54

Why do some families go the route of building a custom home?

    A. They are picky.
    B. They are rich.
    C. They have the time.
    D. They have many needs.
    E. They like construction work.

Answer:

QUESTION 55

Which of the following can be inferred from the passage?

A. All Americans eventually own a home.
B. Some Americans give up on owning a home.
C. Trade offs are required when buying a home.
D. Home buying is a simple process.
E. Building a custom home can be easy.

Answer:

Having a vision is absolutely necessary to ensure success in life. Vision allows us to set goals, and we strive to reach those goals. Reaching the goals might result in some difficulties, but we must endure the obstacles to reach the vision of success.

QUESTION 56

According to the passage, to be successful one must:

A. ensure obstacles
B. set goals
C. reach goals
D. have a vision
E. vision success

Answer:

This page is intentionally left blank.

Exam Key – Practice Exam 1

Question Number	Correct Answer	Question Number	Correct Answer
1	A	29	B
2	C	30	D
3	E	31	A
4	C	32	D
5	D	33	D
6	B	34	C
7	A	35	B
8	C	36	A
9	B	37	B
10	D	38	D
11	D	39	A
12	A	40	D
13	A	41	C
14	B	42	C
15	D	43	A
16	A	44	D
17	C	45	D
18	C	46	B
19	C	47	E
20	D	48	B
21	E	49	C
22	D	50	C
23	A	51	C
24	A	52	C
25	A	53	C
26	C	54	D
27	D	55	B
28	B	56	D

NOTE: Getting approximately 80% of the questions correct increases chances of obtaining passing score on the real exam. This varies from different states and university programs.

This page is intentionally left blank.

Reading Practice Exam 1 – Questions and Explanations

Written by Simon J. Barrington

When charged with a crime, one option is to plea out the charge. A plea bargain is an arrangement between a defendant and a prosecutor, in which the defendant agrees to plead guilty or no contest. Most lawyers push clients toward a plea bargain, so they do not have to spend a lot of time on the case.

QUESTION 1

Which of the following is an unstated assumption made in the statement?

- A. plea bargains are the best options to a speedy conclusion
- B. lawyers make easy money by pushing plea bargains
- C. defendants have to agree to the plea bargains
- D. plea bargains are very common
- E. plea bargains are easy to get

Answer: A

Explanation: The excerpt states that "they do not have to spend a lot of time on the case," so they don't have to spend a lot of time for the case. The situation ends faster than going to trail.

Written by Elizabeth Cady Stanton

I urge a sixteenth amendment, because "manhood suffrage," or a man's government, is civil, religious, and social disorganization. The male element is a destructive force, stern, selfish, aggrandizing, loving war, violence, conquest, acquisition, breeding in the material and moral world alike discord, disorder, disease, and death. See what a record of blood and cruelty the pages of history reveal! Through what slavery, slaughter, and sacrifice, through what inquisitions and imprisonments, pains and persecutions, black codes and gloomy creeds, the soul of humanity has struggled for the centuries, while mercy has veiled her face and all hearts have been dead alike to love and hope!

QUESTION 2

The passage uses words that start with the same letters (ex. material and moral, discord, disorder, disease, and death, slavery, slaughter, and sacrifice, inquisitions and imprisonments, and pains and persecutions). What is the purpose of doing so?

- A. it is common practice
- B. shows exaggerations
- C. grabs the readers' attention
- D. shows the importance of the topic
- E. shows the need for the amendment

Answer: C

Explanation: When someone is reading the paragraph, the words that start with the same letters will capture the readers' attention.

QUESTION 3

Which of the following best describes the tone of the passage?

- A. regret
- B. negative
- C. appealing
- D. incepting
- E. intolerable

Answer: E

Explanation: The writer is using bold and harsh words. The tone of the passage is unbearable, insufferable, and intolerable.

QUESTION 4

What is the purpose of the paragraph?

- A. to explain the horrors of society
- B. to convey that despite horror in society there is hope
- C. to get an amendment ratified
- D. manhood suffrage is the cause of problems
- E. people have died for love and hope

Answer: C

Explanation: The passage starts with "I urge a sixteenth amendment." The purpose is to get an amendment passed.

Written by Anonymous Author

In America, majority of children attend elementary and secondary public institutions in which they spend approximately seven hours, on average, of their day in school. During school, children eat two meals along with snacks. Having vending machines selling unhealthy snacks, such as sodas and processed snack foods, have prompted some debate. Unhealthy foods are major cause of obesity, diabetes, and heart disease, and school institutions promote the idea of good health, so to place vending machines in school corridors is hypocritical of school leaders. Vending machines with unhealthy options should not be allowed on school properties.

With students spending more time in school than with their parents, schools have a responsibility to convey an <u>incontrovertible</u> message regarding good eating habits. Schools are a very influential force in developing young people's minds. Most schools require health education, in which students are conveyed the message of the benefits of fruits and vegetables, fiber, and protein…Schools are an institution with authority, similar to parents. If a father constantly gave his son a lunch of Lay's chips and a Coca Cola, he would be considered a bad father, especially if the child suffered health complications. Institutions that are allowed to have unhealthy options in vending machines are similarly negligent…

Giving students the option to use healthy vending machines supports the growing problems associated with junk food, such as obesity, diabetes, heart disease, and laziness…Individuals who are obese might not feel very happy with their appearance. This is especially true when looking at the number of surgical options individuals undertake to reduce the weight on their body. In addition, treating heart disease, stroke, and diabetes is expensive. In order to effectively initiate solving the problem, schools have to be involved in establishing the idea of good eating habits at a young age. Providing healthier options in public schools will not only reduce obesity among children, but it will also give the children energy they need. Teachers often encounter students' laziness, tiredness, and sleepiness especially in the afternoon due to heavy food intake. Offering healthier food options will give the students the energy they need to go through the afternoon sessions. The negative impact of processed foods and sodas is significant, and schools don't need to have vending machines to be <u>enablers</u> of the problem associated with unhealthy eating.

The students of our public schools are the future of our society, so schools need to ensure individuals have healthy options to eat to reduce the chances of obesity, diabetes, and heart disease. Vending machines selling junk food have no place where students go to be educated.

QUESTION 5

Which of the following most weaken the argument of the passage?

- A. Parents are more responsible of what students eat.
- B. Students should have the right to choose what to eat.
- C. Some individuals have medical problems that require them to eat sugary snacks.
- D. Students who want unhealthy snacks can find it outside of school.
- E. Discussing eating healthy options in health education classes covers school responsibilities.

Answer: D

Explanation: The passage discusses how schools have a responsibility to promote healthy options. Option D is true and weakens the argument of the passage.

QUESTION 6

Which of the following is the strongest statement from the passage that supports the idea of banning unhealthy vending machines?

- A. Schools have a responsibility not only to teach students the importance of eating healthy but also to practice that message.
- B. Giving students the option to use healthy vending machines supports the growing problems associated with junk food, such as obesity, diabetes, heart disease, and laziness.
- C. With students spending more time in school than with their parents, schools have a responsibility to convey an incontrovertible message regarding good eating habits.
- D. Vending machines selling junk food have no place where students go to be educated.
- E. When schools are allowed to have vending machines that sell sodas and snack foods, the message of eating healthy is contradicted.

Answer: B

Explanation: Options D not reasons for banning unhealthy vending machines. Option A and E are not stated in the passage. Option B is a reason for banning unhealthy vending machines and the strongest statement of all options. Option C is not as strong as Option B as Option B discusses possible health problems.

QUESTION 7

Which of the following best explains the relationship between the following two sentences?

Sentence 1: Schools are an institution with authority, similar to parents.

Sentence 2: If a father constantly gave his son a lunch of Lay's chips and a Coca Cola, he would be considered a bad father, especially if the child suffered health complications.

   A. Sentence 2 is an example that relates to the statement in Sentence 1.
   B. Sentence 2 provides validation to Sentence 1.
   C. Sentence 2 strengthens the statement in Sentence 1.
   D. Sentence 2 is similar to Sentence 1.
   E. Sentence 2 expands on the idea of Sentence 1.

Answer: A

Explanation: Sentence 1 states that schools are similar to parents. Sentence 2 provides an example that relates to the statement in Sentence 1.

QUESTION 8

Which of the following negative consequences is not directly mentioned regarding junk food?

   A. tiredness
   B. heart disease
   C. bad grades
   D. sleepiness
   E. laziness

Answer: C

Explanation: Bad grades were not directly mentioned as a consequence of junk food.

QUESTION 9

Which of the following best describes the purpose of the first passage?

   A. Inform readers that vending machines with junk food is a problem in public institutions.
   B. Take a firm stand against having vending machines on school properties.
   C. Inform readers that healthy food options are absolutely necessary.
   D. Discuss the time students spend in school.
   E. Communicate the different aspects of junk foods.

Answer: B

Explanation: The first paragraph discusses the negative aspects of vending machines with unhealthy options. The writer is taking a firm stand against vending machines on school properties, and the statement: "Vending machines with unhealthy options should not be allowed on school properties" confirms the writer's position.

QUESTION 10

From the passage, it can be inferred that healthy foods will

   A. eliminate diabetes and heart diseases.
   B. help promote a better image for schools.
   C. give more options for students during lunch.
   D. help students in the classroom.
   E. eliminate obesity in schools across the nation.

Answer: D

Explanation: The passage states that students can be "laziness, tiredness, and sleepiness." As a result, having healthy food options will help students in the classroom.

QUESTION 11

Which of the following is the most appropriate replacement word for enablers?

- A. blowers
- B. captures
- C. detractor
- D. promoters
- E. supporters

Answer: D

Explanation: The sentence uses the word "enablers" as allowing something to happen. The best replacement word is promoters.

QUESTION 12

Which of the following best explains the relationship between the two sentences?

Sentence 1: Vending machines with unhealthy options should not be allowed on school properties.

Sentence 2: Vending machines selling junk food have no place where students go to be educated.

- A. Sentence 1 is a thesis statement and Sentence 2 is a repetitive form of Sentence 1.
- B. Sentence 2 is an example that relates to the statement in Sentence 1.
- C. Sentence 2 strengthens the statement in Sentence 1.
- D. Sentence 2 provides validation to Sentence 1.
- E. Sentence 2 expands on the idea of Sentence 1.

Answer: A

Explanation: Sentence 1 is the thesis statement and Sentence 2 is repetitive form of Sentence 1. Sentence 2 is concluding sentence to the passage.

QUESTION 13

Which of the following can be added to the passage to strengthen the position?

    A. Obesity, diabetes, and heart diseases have caused countless lives in America.
    B. Schools have greater responsibilities than parents as students spend more time in school.
    C. Junk food has many harmful ingredients that are hurtful to children.
    D. All doctors recommend having healthy options in school to eat.
    E. None of the above

Answer: A

Explanation: Obesity, diabetes, and heart diseases are mentioned multiple times, so indicating that obesity, diabetes, and heart diseases have caused countless lives in America will strengthen the position taken.

QUESTION 14

What is the meaning of incontrovertible?

    A. questionable
    B. incontestable
    C. correct
    D. acceptable
    E. arguable

Answer: B

Explanation: The meaning of incontrovertible is incontestable; meaning that there is no question regarding the statement.

Source One

Written by Asa Gace Benetton

In recent years, Indiana has seen a sharp decline in new teachers entering into the classroom. Between 2008 and 2015, Indiana has seen about a 30 percent decline in the number of first-time teacher licenses being given by the Indiana Department of Education. In fact, comparing data from 2014 and 2015, the number of licenses issued to first-time teachers was down 21 percent. The lack of interest in becoming a teacher is the result of a decade long decline in enrollment in education programs in some major universities in Indiana. The shortage of teachers in Indiana has become so significant that is has been raised to the state legislature. Public officials are proposing solutions such as discussing more about the teaching profession with young adults, creating more education classes, and seeking out teachers of diverse background…

Others indicate that the new teacher certification examinations are the cause of teachers being swayed from perusing teaching careers. Some potential teachers have taken the exam multiple times and have changed career paths due to having difficulty passing the certification exams. Many also blame the implementation of the Common Core State Standards in 2014, which made it harder to deliver quality education. As a result, the teaching profession has obtained a negative perception. Only time will tell if the proposed solution will solve the problem of teacher shortage in Indiana.

Source Two

Written by Leonard Jacob Farmington

Most States across the nation are seeing shortages in teachers, including California. For the last couple of years, California has seen a major decline in issuing teaching certifications, and districts are forced to scramble to fill those positions. California is the most populated State in the United States, but is one of the States with the least amount of certified teachers. For example, California ranks the lowest with high student-to-teacher ratios; the State would need 100,000 additional teachers right now to bring that ratio down to the national average. Moreover, according to the Center for the Future of Teaching and Learning, California will need about an additional 100,000 teachers over the next decade…

Experts claim that recruitment of teachers in the State has declined to the lowest in history, and efforts made to retain qualified teachers have declined. The salaries of teachers are a lot less than salaries of other professions that require <u>comparable</u> education, training, and skills. With the rising cost of living, it is harder for individuals to initiate or continue pursuing a teaching career.

QUESTION 15

Passage 1 indicates creating more education classes as one solution

- A. to get students informed about education.
- B. to help potential teachers in gaining best practices.
- C. to help potential teachers on new teacher certification exams.
- D. to get students more interested in education.
- E. to give more opportunities to get teaching degree.

Answer: D

Explanation: The first paragraph talks about the lack of interest of students related to undertaking an education career path. The last sentence of the first paragraph discusses the solutions related to the lack of interest.

QUESTION 16

Which of the following best describes the relationship between Sentence 1 and 2?

Sentence 1: Between 2008 and 2015, Indiana has seen about a 30 percent decline in the number of first-time teacher licenses being given by the Indiana Department of Education.

Sentence 2: The lack of interest in becoming a teacher is the result of a decade long decline in enrollment in education programs in some major universities in Indiana.

- A. Sentence 2 provides a possible reason supporting Sentence 1.
- B. Sentence 2 contradicts Sentence 1.
- C. Sentence 1 provides counterargument for Sentence 2.
- D. Sentence 1 gives an example of problem mentioned in Sentence 2.
- E. Sentence 2 provides data for Sentence 1.

Answer: A

Explanation: Sentence 1 indicates a decline in number of first time teacher licenses, and Sentence 2 gives a possible reason for the decline in licenses.

QUESTION 17

It can be inferred that teaching certification exams are harder because

- A. of updated standards.
- B. of lack of good education program.
- C. of the Common Core State Standards.
- D. of the lack of interest.
- E. of the shortage of teachers

Answer: C

Explanation: Teaching certification exams are harder because of "the implementation of the Common Core State Standards."

QUESTION 18

Which of the following statements can weaken Passage 1 position?

- A. The shortage of teachers will eventually be solved.
- B. Some individuals have a positive perception for the teaching profession.
- C. In 2014 and 2015, more individuals changed their careers to be teachers.
- D. Changes in teacher certification exams are the main reasons for shortage of changes.
- E. Common Core State Standards did help some schools in the United States in improving math skills.

Answer: C

Explanation: Passage 1 position is surrounding the idea of teacher shortage in Indiana, so indicating more individuals changed their career to the education field in 2014 and 2015 will weaken the position of Passage 1.

QUESTION 19

According to Passage 2, which of the following is not a reason for teacher shortage?

- A. recruitment
- B. salaries
- C. training
- D. cost of living
- E. retention

Answer: C

Explanation: Recruitment and retention are reasons for teacher shortage mentioned in the first sentence of the second paragraph. Salaries are also mentioned in the second paragraph along with cost of living. Training is not a reason for teacher shortage mentioned in Passage 2.

QUESTION 20

Which of the following is an acceptable replacement for the word comparable?

- A. similar
- B. equivalent
- C. identical
- D. the same level
- E. duplicate

Answer: D

Explanation: Option A, C, D, and E indicate that education is the exact same. However, option D indicates same level, which is the most appropriate replacement.

QUESTION 21

Which of the following is a common reason for teacher shortage in both passages?

- A. salaries
- B. training
- C. retention
- D. living cost
- E. recruitment

Answer: E

Explanation: Both passages indicate recruitment as a reason for teacher shortages. Passage 1 states: "The lack of interest in becoming a teacher is the result of a decade long decline in enrollment in education programs in some major universities in Indiana." Passage 2 states: "Experts claim that recruitment of teachers in the State has declined to the lowest in history, and efforts made to retain qualified teachers have declined."

QUESTION 22

Both passages present all the following except?

- A. numerical data
- B. possible solutions
- C. reasons for the problem
- D. public officials finding solutions
- E. example of problems faced in States

Answer: D

Explanation: Both passages present numerical data, possible solutions to teacher shortage problems, and reasons for teacher shortage problems. Passage 1 discusses the State of Indiana, and Passage 2 discusses the State of California. Only Passage 1 discusses public officials getting involved.

QUESTION 23

Passage 2 presents a weaker position than Passage 1 for teacher shortage because

- A. California has a larger population, so teacher shortage issue is something that is more likely.
- B. California does not have public officials involved in implementing solutions.
- C. California needs a lot more teachers over the next decade.
- D. the cost of living is contributing to teacher shortage.
- E. districts are forced to scramble to fill those positions.

Answer: A

Explanation: With California being the most populated state, the idea of teacher shortage is not shocking. Passage 2 has a weak argument than Passage 1 regarding teacher shortage. Indiana is a lesser populated state that should not see teacher shortage but does.

QUESTION 24

Based on both passages, it can be inferred that

- A. the problem of teacher shortage is being addressed in both States.
- B. recruitment is the key to solving the problem of teacher shortage.
- C. the problem of teacher shortage will never be solved.
- D. the problem of teacher shortage has always been in existence.
- E. the problem of teacher shortage is the most critical issue in both Indiana and California.

Answer: A

Explanation: Option B is not something to infer as it is stated directly in each of the passages. There is nothing to suggest Option C, D, and E can be inferred. Both passages acknowledged the problems and possible solutions, so the problem of teacher shortage is being addressed in both States.

QUESTION 25

Which of the following sentence from Passage 1 can best be placed at the end of the second paragraph of Passage 2?

A. As a result, the teaching profession has obtained a negative perception.
B. Many also blame the implementation of the Common Core State Standards in 2014, which made it harder to deliver quality education.
C. Others indicate that the new teacher certification examinations are the cause of teachers being swayed from perusing teaching careers.
D. In fact, comparing data from 2014 and 2015, the number of licenses issued to first-time teachers was down 21 percent.
E. Public officials are proposing solutions such as discussing more about the teaching profession with young adults, creating more education classes, and seeking out teachers of diverse background.

Answer: A

Explanation: Passage 2 does not provide a positive tone; Passage 2 can indicate a negative perception of the teaching profession. Option A is the best option that fits well with the content of Passage 2.

Written by Lord Chesterfield

THERE is no branch of a man's education, no portion of his intercourse with other men, and no quality which will stand him in good stead more frequently than the capability of writing a good letter upon any and every subject. In business, in his intercourse with society, in, I may say, almost every circumstance of his life, he will find his pen called into requisition. Yet, although so important, so almost indispensable an accomplishment, it is one which is but little cultivated, and a letter, perfect in every part, is a great rarity.

In the composition of a good letter there are many points to be considered, and we take first the simplest and lowest, namely, the spelling.

Many spell badly from ignorance, but more from carelessness. The latter, writing rapidly, make, very often, mistakes that would disgrace a schoolboy. If you are in doubt about a word, do not from a feeling of false shame let the spelling stand in its doubtful position hoping that, if wrong, it will pass unnoticed, but get a dictionary, and see what is the correct orthography. Besides the actual misplacing of letters in a word there is another fault of careless, rapid writing, frequently seen. This is to write two words in one, running them together. I have more than once seen with him written withim, and for her stand thus, forer. Strange, too, as it may seem, it is more frequently the short, common words that are misspelled than long ones. They flow from the pen mechanically, while over an unaccustomed word the writer unconsciously stops to consider the orthography. Chesterfield, in his advice to his son, says:

"I come now to another part of your letter, which is the orthography, if I may call bad spelling orthography. You spell induce, enduce; and grandeur, you spell grandure; two faults of which few of my housemaids would have been guilty. I must tell you that orthography, in the true sense of the word, is so absolutely necessary for a man of letters, or a gentleman, that one false spelling may fix ridicule upon him for the rest of his life; and I know a man of quality, who never recovered the ridicule of having spelled wholesome without the w.

QUESTION 26

What is the main idea expressed in the passage?

- A. using the right orthography is important in writing
- B. it is important to write a good letter
- C. correct spelling of the English language is vital
- D. it is important to watch out for careless mistakes
- E. writing is important for obtaining good education

Answer: C

Explanation: Option A is indicated in the last paragraph, but is not the main idea. The main idea is not the importance of writing a good letter, so Option B is incorrect. Option D is expressed in the passage, but not the main idea. Option is E is not related to the passage. Option C is the main idea of the passage.

QUESTION 27

What is the purpose of the passage?

- A. watch out for careless mistakes
- B. know how to write a letter
- C. explain the process of writing a letter
- D. convey the reader that spelling is important
- E. let his son know that orthography is important

Answer: D

Explanation: The purpose of the passage is to convey to the reader that spelling is important. This is expressed throughout the passage.

QUESTION 28

Which of the following best describes the organization pattern of the passage?

A. importance
B. process
C. chronological
D. topical
E. problem-solution

Answer: B

Explanation: This statement "In the composition of a good letter there are many points to be considered, and we take first the simplest and lowest, namely, the spelling" indicates a process approach is being used. Chronological pattern is more used when dealing with events.

QUESTION 29

This passage shows bias in favor of:

A. writing letters
B. traditional spelling of the English language
C. using correct wording
D. non-educated writers
E. using dictionary

Answer: B

Explanation: The writer of the passage mentions using correct orthography, which is the conventional spelling system of a language.

QUESTION 30

What is the tone of this passage?

- A. negative
- B. positive
- C. conservative
- D. earnest
- E. honest

Answer: D

Explanation: The passage does not take a negative or a positive tone. Option C and E are not related to the passage tone. The passage has an earnest tone.

QUESTION 31

Which of the following can be inferred from the passage?

- A. disagreement exists over whether traditional or phonetic spelling is preferable
- B. spelling errors can happen on common words used regularly
- C. a good letter must be error free of spelling mistakes
- D. the writer is trying to make the letter personal to his son
- E. using the right orthography is critical for good spelling

Answer: A

Explanation: Options B, C, and E are directly stated in the passage and not something one needs to infer. Option D is not accurate. Option A is an inference that can be made based on the last paragraph.

QUESTION 32

Enrollment of Students at Bunker Hill University - 2005

	Males	Females	Total
College of Business	250	300	550
College of Engineering	162	85	247
College of Liberal Arts	144	225	369
College of Natural Sciences	325	336	661
College of Technology	114	96	210

The table above shows enrollment of students in different college departments at the Bunker Hill University in 2005. Which conclusion about enrollment at the Bunker Hill University is best supported by the table?

A. The College of Natural Sciences had the most number of enrollments in 2015.
B. Bunker Hill University is not seeing decline in enrollment.
C. Bunker Hill University has satisfied enrollment requirements for 2005.
D. The College of Natural Sciences has greater chance of having more male enrollment than female in the future.
E. The College of Engineering has greater chance of having more female enrollment than male in the future.

Answer: D

Explanation: The table shows that the College of Natural Sciences has 325 male students and 336 female students. The numbers are very close, so there is a greater chance of having more male enrollment than female in the future at the College of Natural Sciences.

Written by Anonymous Author

In America, education has long been considered a priceless and enduring asset. However, when this benefit is deliberately being denied, actions must be undertaken to defend his or her educational rights. History does indeed portray this idea, particularly the case of Brown v. Board of Education of Topeka, Kansas. This class action lawsuit is believed to be one of the most important decisions of the Supreme Court. Basically, the case was a milestone in the innovation of outlawing segregation in public schools because segregation violated the Equal Protection Clause of the Fourteenth Amendment. The decision of the courts intensified the hope and faith of many African Americans. The decision was a key to encouraging more people to take a stand for their rights. To this day, the Supreme Court ruling undoubtedly has an immeasurable impact on the lives of countless African Americans. Today, African Americans can attend any public school and sit across from whites, without any racial discrimination.

QUESTION 33

From the passage, which of the following can be interpreted as not completely accurate?

- A. Education is considered an enduring asset.
- B. Brown v. Board of Education of Topeka, Kansas had a huge impact in America.
- C. Equal Protection Clause of the Fourteenth Amendment supported the decision made by the Supreme Court.
- D. African Americans can attend any public school without any racial discrimination.
- E. Taking a stand can results in a change.

Answer: D

Explanation: Stating that African Americans can attend any public school without any racial discrimination maybe challenged. To this day, some individuals might experience racial discrimination in public institutions.

QUESTION 34

What is a better replacement word for innovation?

A. notion
B. creation
C. efforts
D. plight
E. improvement

Answer: C

Explanation: Replacing innovation with efforts fits well with the context of the sentence. Basically, the case was a milestone in the efforts of outlawing segregation in public schools because segregation violated the Equal Protection Clause of the Fourteenth Amendment.

QUESTION 35

What is the relationship between these two sentences?

Sentence 1: In America, education has long been considered a priceless and enduring asset.

Sentence 2: To this day, the Supreme Court ruling undoubtedly has an immeasurable impact on the lives of countless African Americans.

A. Sentence 2 analyzes the comment in sentence 1.
B. Sentence 1 provides support to the information in sentence 2.
C. Sentence 2 explains the main idea of sentence 1.
D. Sentence 1 defines education and sentence 2 provides an impact.
E. Sentence 2 counters the main idea of sentence 1.

Answer: B

Explanation: Sentence 1 explains how education is a long term asset while sentence 2 explains the impact of the Supreme Court ruling to be endless on the lives of African Americans. Sentence 1 supports the information in sentence 2.

Written by Anonymous Author

In my opinion, much of the real estate troubles have come from the sub-prime market, meaning buyers were getting in over their heads. Either they did not put down sufficient down payments or their debt ratios were out of line. What may have happened is that banks and mortgage companies were seeking continued growth and began creating additional programs for this sub-prime market, such as interest -- only and other more aggressive programs -- many with adjustable rates. This created a larger pool of people who were able to afford homes. However, many of these buyers have marginal credit worthiness and have now begun to fall behind on mortgage payments, taxes, and credit card payments, which fueled the foreclosure crisis.

As anyone in the real estate business knows, the housing market is cyclical: as interest rates drop, the housing market picks up, and as interest rates rise, the apartment rental market picks up. The commercial market, which includes apartment complexes, should begin to see a decrease in vacancy and an increase in rental income in the apartment sector. People need a place to live and most people facing foreclosure will need to rent houses or apartments. As for the outlook for next year, I think the meltdown is not as dire as the media reports. People still need a place to live, thus, as long as unemployment stays low in most areas, next year should probably see real estate prices decline slightly. Housing prices will level off and drop in some of the condo markets such as Florida, Arizona, Vegas and parts of the Carolinas. As for the rest of the country, I foresee a cooling period with modest gains in value over the next couple of years. But, then again, who knows for certain what will happen?

The increase in foreclosure properties does benefit consumers and will probably impact the real estate market positively. I believe that with the rise in foreclosures, middle class families will take advantage of foreclosure properties because they cost much less. Even though foreclosed homes need some repairs, the benefits outweigh the costs. When my family purchased a foreclosed house, we repaired the damages ourselves. We painted all the walls, replaced tiles, and repaired other minor damage, and it only cost $1,000, as opposed to hiring a contractor, which would have cost $6,000.

Education and immigration can significantly impact the housing market. With more people obtaining higher education, income will substantially increase, making buying a house a much easier task. According to the "Housing Opportunities in Foreign-Born Market," since 1995 immigrants contribute to one-third of the household growth in the United States. Immigrants, who become U.S. citizens, own homes at substantially higher rates than non-citizens across all age groups. Looking at the history of immigrants in reference to real estate and today's increase in immigration rates, leads me to believe that perhaps investments in residential properties will increase.

People will always possess the desire to own a home. A lovely family, a good job, and a wonderful house portray the American dream. In my opinion, since many people strive to make their dream a reality, the housing market will certainly not suffer a severe blow over the next year or even in the long run.

QUESTION 36

The tone of this passage could best be described as

- A. optimistic
- B. harsh
- C. critical
- D. cunning
- E. helpful

Answer: A

Explanation: The passage provides information on how the housing market is cyclical. There are good times and harder times. However, overall, the passage provides hope that the housing market will be strong. The tone of the passage is optimistic.

QUESTION 37

One can infer that the housing market is

- A. not going to survive one day.
- B. going to survive harsh times.
- C. going to require many architects.
- D. going to be lucrative due to condos.
- E. always going to be a sub-prime market.

Answer: B

Explanation: The passage provides information that indicates the housing market is going to survive the difficult times.

QUESTION 38

- I. sub-prime market
- II. low down payment
- III. insufficient debt ratios
- IV. immigration

Of the above, which of the following contributed to the foreclosure crisis?

- A. I and II
- B. I and III
- C. I, II, and IV
- D. I, II, and III
- E. I, II, III, and IV

Answer: D

Explanation: The first paragraph indicates the reasons that contributed to the foreclosure crisis.

QUESTION 39

Which of the following best describes what the passage is conveying?

A. The passage is conveying the reasons for the foreclosure crisis, condition of the current market, and future outlook of the housing market.
B. The passage is conveying the factors that contribute to the strength of the housing market.
C. The passage is conveying the importance of the housing market and understanding the foreclosure crisis.
D. The passage is conveying the different reasons for the foreclosure crisis.
E. The passage is conveying the future outlook of the housing market.

Answer: A

Explanation: The passage discusses the reasons for the foreclosure crisis. The passage also discusses the current market conditions along with the outlook of the housing market.

QUESTION 40

Which of the following is best to evaluate the validity of the author's claim regarding Florida, Arizona, Vegas and parts of the Carolinas?

A. Provide an example of housing prices leveling off in another State.
B. Provide an example of housing prices leveling off and dropping in the condo markets from 10 years ago.
C. Provide explanation of possible future leveling off and dropping in the condo markets.
D. Provide example of data or study from at least one State showing the possible leveling off and dropping in the condo markets.
E. Provide details of which cities exactly will level off and drop in condo markets.

Answer: D

Explanation: The passage is stating that housing prices will level off and drop in some of the condo markets such as Florida, Arizona, Vegas and parts of the Carolinas. To validate this claim, the best option is to provide example of data or study from at least one State regarding the leveling off and dropping in the condo markets. This will provide back-up evidence to the claim.

QUESTION 41

According to the passage, who benefits the most when there is a foreclosure crisis?

- A. banks
- B. investors
- C. middle class families
- D. immigrants
- E. low-income families

Answer: C

Explanation: The passage states the following: "The increase in foreclosure properties does benefit consumers and will probably impact the real estate market positively. I believe that with the rise in foreclosures, middle class families will take advantage of foreclosure properties because they cost much less." Middle class families will benefit the most.

QUESTION 42

What is the purpose of using personal experience in paragraph 5?

    A. to strengthen the argument
    B. to establish a personal connection
    C. to give an example of how foreclosure property can be financially beneficial
    D. to explain how foreclosure property can be repaired
    E. to explain the importance of getting a foreclosure property

Answer: C

Explanation: The paragraph talks about the advantages of foreclosure properties, so the example is to explain how foreclosure property can be financially beneficial.

QUESTION 43

What is the relationship between Sentence 1 and Sentence 2?

Sentence 1: Looking at the history of immigrants in reference to real estate and today's increase in immigration rates, leads me to believe that perhaps investments in residential properties will increase.

Sentence 2: In my opinion, since many people strive to make their dream a reality, the housing market will certainly not suffer a severe blow over the next year or even in the long run.

    A. Sentence 1 supports the statement in Sentence 2.
    B. Sentence 1 explains the statement in Sentence 2.
    C. Sentence 1 weakens the statement in Sentence 2.
    D. Sentence 1 expands the statement in Sentence 2.
    E. Sentence 1 and Sentence 2 do not have a relationship.

Answer: A

Explanation: Sentence 2 talks about how the housing market will certainly not suffer a severe blow over the next year or even in the long run, and Sentence 1 talks about how immigration contributes to housing market. Sentence 1 is supporting Sentence 2's idea of housing marking being strong.

QUESTION 44

What is the purpose of the following statement: "But, then again, who knows for certain what will happen?"

- A. housing market is gaining strength
- B. the author's confidence is low
- C. there are many interpretation for the housing market
- D. housing market is a very fickle area
- E. housing market has a path forward

Answer: D

Explanation: The statement is conveying that the housing market is not certain, so the purpose of the statement is to indicate that the hosing marking is a fickle area.

QUESTION 45

What is the purpose of the sixth paragraph?

- A. to give reason for why the housing market can be cyclical
- B. to give information on factors that impact the housing market
- C. to provide data related to the housing market
- D. to strength the argument that the housing market can survive in the long run
- E. to convey immigrants can contribute to the housing market

Answer: D

Explanation: The purpose of the sixth paragraph is to strengthen the argument that the housing market can survive in the long run. Options B and E are information provided in the paragraph, but does not communicate the purpose.

QUESTION 46

What is a common solution mentioned in the passage when individuals are faced with foreclosure?

- A. selling their homes
- B. renting a property
- C. refinancing existing loan
- D. getting a condo
- E. getting another loan

Answer: B

Explanation: The passage states: "People need a place to live and most people facing foreclosure will need to rent houses or apartments." The common solution when individuals are faced with foreclosure is renting a property.

Written by Benjamin Banneker to Thomas Jefferson, framer of the Declaration of Independence

Sir, suffer me to recall to your mind that time in which the arms and tyranny of the British Crown were exerted with every powerful effort in order to reduce you to a State of Servitude, look back I entreat you on the variety of dangers to which you were exposed; reflect on that time in which every human aid appeared unavailable, and in which even hope and fortitude wore the aspect of inability to the conflict…

This sir, was a time in which you clearly saw into the injustice of a state of slavery and in which you had just apprehensions of the horrors of its condition, it was now, sir, that your abhorrence thereof was so excited, that you publickly held forth this true and valuable doctrine, which is worthy to be recorded and remembered in all succeeding ages. "We hold these truths to be self-evident, that all men are created equal, and that they are endowed by their creator with certain unalienable rights, that among these are life, liberty and the pursuit of happiness." [Declaration of Independence]

Here, sir, was a time in which your tender feelings for yourselves had engaged you thus to declare, you were then impressed with proper ideas of the great valuation of liberty and the free possession of those blessings to which you were entitled by nature…you should at the same time counteract his mercies in detaining by fraud and violence so numerous a part of my brethren under groaning captivity and cruel oppression, that you should at the same time be found guilty of that most criminal act which you professedly detested in others with respect to yourselves.

QUESTION 47

I. he does not want to antagonize Jefferson
II. reason with Jefferson
III. has utmost respect for Jefferson
IV. destroys the possible notion that race makes people inferior

Of the above, why does Banneker use the word "Sir" multiple times?

A. I and II
B. I and III
C. I, II, and III
D. I, II, and IV
E. I, II, III, and IV

Answer: E

Explanation: Banneker wants to state his opinion, so he uses "Sir" to reason with Jefferson and show sign of respect. It is also that Banneker is not perceived to antagonize Jefferson. Most importantly, repeating "Sir" shows Jefferson that Banneker is a dignified person, which destroys possible notion that race makes people inferior.

QUESTION 48

What is the purpose of the letter?

- A. communicate the horror of slavery
- B. argue against slavery
- C. argue against tyranny
- D. bring about change to society
- E. bring about kindness to the world

Answer: B

Explanation: Option A is something the writer does in the letter, but is not the main purpose. The writer is not arguing against tyranny or bring about kindness to the world. The writer wants to see change in society, but the purpose is to argue against slavery.

QUESTION 49

What is the strength of using the quote "We hold these truths to be self-evident, that all men are created equal, and that they are endowed by their creator with certain unalienable rights, that among these are life, liberty and the pursuit of happiness."?

- A. the quote is indicating that all men are equal
- B. the quote is important in American history
- C. the quote is written by Jefferson himself
- D. the quote indicates individuals should be happy
- E. the quote is good example of how life should be in America

Answer: C

Explanation: Banneker is discussing the horror of slavery and uses a quote from Jefferson to show how society should be. Using a quote that Jefferson himself wrote shows strength in Banneker's argument.

QUESTION 50

What is the tone of the second paragraph?

A. neutral
B. bias
C. dark
D. disinterested
E. pale

Answer: C

Explanation: The tone is dark as it states "the injustice of state of slavery" and "horrors of its conditions."

QUESTION 51

Which of the following quotes from the letter might Jefferson disagree or dislike the most?

A. "Sir, suffer me to recall to your mind that time in which the arms and tyranny of the British Crown were exerted with every powerful effort in order to reduce you to a State of Servitude…"
B. "…the present freedom and tranquility which you enjoy you have mercifully received and that it is the peculiar blessing of Heaven."
C. "…that you should at the same time be found guilty of that most criminal act which you professedly detested in others with respect to yourselves."
D. "…how pitiable is it to reflect that although you were so fully convinced of the benevolence of the Father of mankind…"
E. "…Job proposed to his friends, "put your souls in their souls stead," thus shall your hearts be enlarged with kindness and benevolence towards them…"

Answer: C

Explanation: Jefferson will likely most disagree with Option C as it puts blame on him and states that he committed a criminal act.

QUESTION 52

Benjamin Banneker describes slavery as all the following except:

A. injustice
B. horror
C. danger
D. cruel
E. criminal

Answer: C

Explanation: Banneker uses the word danger to describe the arms and tyranny of the British Crown. All other options Banneker used to describe slavery.

Written by Anonymous Author

The American dream that many strive to reach is to own a home. Finding a home can be a very challenging endeavor as it takes some individuals' months to even years to get a home. From deciding location to square feet to interior designs to cost, families have to weigh the various options and make some trades to be able to settle on a dream home. Otherwise, the duration of finding a home can be very lengthy to at times even impossible. In fact, the process can be lengthy to the point where it becomes discouraging for some. For most families, buying a home will be done once in their life times, so ensuring that most needs are in the home are critical. Some families who are unable to find existing homes to suit their needs and are wealthy seek options of building a custom home. Custom homes are completely tailored to individual family needs. Going the route of a custom home can be a lengthy and expensive approach; however, some families go this route to reach the American dream. Home buying is not a simple process, but certainly a rewarding process.

QUESTION 53

What is the main idea of the passage?

    A. Home buying is a rewarding process.
    B. Many options exist when it comes to home buying.
    C. Home buying can be a challenging endeavor.
    D. Home buying requires trade off.
    E. Home buying is the American dream.

Answer: C

Explanation: The passage starts with indicating "finding a home can be a very challenging endeavor." Throughout the passage, the theme of home buying being challenging is expressed.

QUESTION 54

Why do some families go the route of building a custom home?

- A. They are picky.
- B. They are rich.
- C. They have the time.
- D. They have many needs.
- E. They like construction work.

Answer: D

Explanation: The passage states: "Some families who are unable to find existing homes to suit their needs and are wealthy seek options of building a custom home. Custom homes are completely tailored to individual family needs." This shows that families that have many needs are unable to find existing homes, so they have to custom build. Option A is not correct as the passage does not indicate individuals who build custom homes are picky.

QUESTION 55

Which of the following can be inferred from the passage?

- A. All Americans eventually own a home.
- B. Some Americans give up on owning a home.
- C. Trade offs are required when buying a home.
- D. Home buying is a simple process.
- E. Building a custom home can be easy.

Answer: B

Explanation: Option A is not indicated in the passage. Option C is true but clearly stated in the passage; not something to infer. Option D and E are not accurate statements. Option B can be inferred from the following statement: "In fact, the process can be lengthy to the point it becomes discouraging for some."

Having a vision is absolutely necessary to ensure success in life. Vision allows us to set goals, and we strive to reach those goals. Reaching the goals might result in some difficulties, but we must endure the obstacles to reach the vision of success.

QUESTION 56

According to the passage, to be successful one must:

- A. ensure obstacles
- B. set goals
- C. reach goals
- D. have a vision
- E. vision success

Answer: D

Explanation: The first sentence clearly states that to be successful, a vision is absolutely necessary.

This page is intentionally left blank.

Practice Test 2

This page is intentionally left blank.

Exam Answer Sheet Test 2

Below is an optional answer sheet to use to document answers.

Question Number	Selected Answer	Question Number	Selected Answer
1		29	
2		30	
3		31	
4		32	
5		33	
6		34	
7		35	
8		36	
9		37	
10		38	
11		39	
12		40	
13		41	
14		42	
15		43	
16		44	
17		45	
18		46	
19		47	
20		48	
21		49	
22		50	
23		51	
24		52	
25		53	
26		54	
27		55	
28		56	

This page is intentionally left blank.

Reading Practice Exam 2 – Questions

Witten by John Down

My dear wife,

I have got a situation in a Factory, in a very pleasant vale about 7 miles from Hudson, and I am to have the whole management of the factory…I was welcome to come to his house at any time; they had on the table pudding, pyes, and fruit of all kind that was in season, and preserves, pickles, vegetables, meat, and everything that a person could wish, and the servants set down at the same table with their masters. They do not think of locking the doors in the country, and you can gather peaches, apples, and all kinds of fruit by the side of the roads. And I can have a barrel of cider holding 32 gallons, for 4s., and they will lend me the barrel till I have emptied it. And I can have 100 lbs. of Beef for 10s… If a man like work he need not want victuals. It is a foolish idea that some people have, that there is too many people come here, it is quite the reverse; there was more than 1000 emigrants came in the day after I landed, and there is four ships have arrived since with emigrants. But there is plenty of room yet, and will for a thousand years to come.

My dear Sukey, all that I want now is to see you, and the dear children here, and then I shall be happy, and not before. You know very well that I should not have left you behind me, if I had money to have took you with me. It was sore against me to do it. But I do not repent of coming, for you know that there was nothing but poverty before me, and to see you and the dear children want was what I could not bear. I would rather cross the Atlantic ten times than hear my children cry for victuals once. Now, my dear, if you can get the Parish to pay for your passage, come directly; for I have not a doubt in my mind I shall be able to keep you in credit. You will find a few inconveniences in crossing the Atlantic, but it will not be long, and when that is over, all is over, for I know that you will like America.

America is not like England, for here no man thinks himself your superior. There is no improper or disgusting equality, for Character has its weight and influence, and the man which is really your superior does not plume himself on being so…There is much attention paid to dress as at any of the watering places in England. Out in the country where I have been you see the young women with their veils and parasols, at the lowest that I saw. Poverty is unknown here…

QUESTION 1

What is the purpose of the letter?

   A. to compare England and America
   B. to convince his wife to come to America
   C. to convince his children to come to America
   D. to explain why he can't come back to live with his family
   E. to explain how much work he has at his job

Answer:

QUESTION 2

Which of the following best characterized the tone in the first paragraph?

   A. serious
   B. colorful
   C. appealing
   D. desperate
   E. personal

Answer:

QUESTION 3

In the passage, why does Down concentrate on everyday household items?

A. to show that America has what England has
B. to show that both countries are partially the same
C. to appeal to his wife to emigrate
D. to appeal to his wife desires to be a housewife
E. to show that they can live the same life in England

Answer:

QUESTION 4

Why did Down go abroad in the first place?

A. to seek opportunities
B. to provide for his family
C. to explore the world
D. to reunite with his parents
E. to live a better life

Answer:

QUESTION 5

Which of the following is an assumption indicated in the passage and Down refutes?

A. America is not the same as England.
B. America is getting crowded.
C. America's wealth is limited.
D. America has everything that a family needs.
E. America is a friendly country.

Answer:

QUESTION 6

Why does Down indicate multiple times that poverty is unknown in America?

A. to show his wife that they can live a life without ever having to worry about being poor
B. to show the magnitude of wealth in America
C. to show that their children will have opportunities
D. to show he lived a poor life prior to coming to America
E. to show how life can change in America

Answer:

QUESTION 7

It can be inferred that Down's wife journey to America might not be possible because?

A. She has never traveled before.
B. She has to come with many children.
C. The trip duration is longer than she has traveled before.
D. She does not have the money to come to America.
E. There are many people trying to come to America.

Answer:

QUESTION 8

What is the meaning of the word plume in the passage?

A. show
B. long
C. pride
D. like
E. influence

Answer:

QUESTION 9

Which of the following is NOT a way Down describes America?

- A. fair
- B. equal
- C. wealthy
- D. spacious
- E. crowded

Answer:

Passage 1

Written by Abraham Lincoln

Let every American, every lover of liberty, every well wisher to his posterity, swear by the blood of the Revolution, never to violate in the least particular, the laws of the country; and never to tolerate their violation by others. As the patriots of seventy-six did to the support of the Declaration of Independence, so to the support of the Constitution and Laws, let every American pledge his life, his property, and his sacred honor;—let every man remember that to violate the law, is to trample on the blood of his father, and to tear the character of his own, and his children's liberty. Let reverence for the laws, be breathed by every American mother, to the lisping babe, that prattles on her lap—let it be taught in schools, in seminaries, and in colleges;—let it be written in Primers, spelling books, and in Almanacs;—let it be preached from the pulpit, proclaimed in legislative halls, and enforced in courts of justice. And, in short, let it become the *political religion* of the nation; and let the old and the young, the rich and the poor, the grave and the gay, of all sexes and tongues, and colors and conditions, sacrifice unceasingly upon its altars. . . .

When I so pressingly urge a strict observance of all the laws, let me not be understood as saying there are no bad laws, nor that grievances may not arise, for the redress of which, no legal provisions have been made. I mean to say no such thing. But I do mean to say, that, although bad laws, if they exist, should be repealed as soon as possible, still while they continue in force, for the sake of example, they should be religiously observed. So also in unprovided cases. If such arise, let proper legal provisions be made for them with the least possible delay; but, till then, let them if not too intolerable, be borne with.

There is no grievance that is a fit object of redress by mob law. In any case that arises, as for instance, the promulgation of abolitionism, one of two positions is necessarily true; that is, the thing is right within itself, and therefore deserves the protection of all law and all good citizens; or, it is wrong, and therefore proper to be prohibited by legal enactments; and in neither case, is the interposition of mob law, either necessary, justifiable, or excusable.

Passage 2

Written by Henry David Thoreau

Unjust laws exist; shall we be content to obey them, or shall we endeavor to amend them, and obey them until we have succeeded, or shall we transgress them at once? Men generally, under such a government as this, think that they ought to wait until they have persuaded the majority to alter them. They think that, if they should resist, the remedy would be worse than the evil. But it is the fault of the government itself that the remedy is worse than the evil. It makes it worse. Why is it not more apt to anticipate and provide for reform? Why does it not cherish its wise minority? Why does it cry and resist before it is hurt? . . .

If the injustice is part of the necessary friction of the machine of government, let it go, let it go; perchance it will wear smooth—certainly the machine will wear out. If the injustice has a spring, or a pulley, or a rope, or a crank, exclusively for itself, then perhaps you may consider whether the remedy will not be worse than the evil; but if it is of such a nature that it requires you to be the agent of injustice to another, then, I say, break the law. Let your life be a counter friction to stop the machine. What I have to do is to see, at any rate, that I do not lend myself to the wrong which I condemn.

As for adopting the ways which the State has provided for remedying the evil, I know not of such ways. They take too much time, and a man's life will be gone. I have other affairs to attend to. I came into this world, not chiefly to make this a good place to live in, but to live in it, be it good or bad. A man has not everything to do, but something; and because he cannot do everything, it is not necessary that he should do something wrong. . . .

QUESTION 10

What is the main idea of the first paragraph of Passage 1?

    A. Laws are important to the United States of America.
    B. Following the law is a necessity for all Americans.
    C. Disobeying the law will result in consequences.
    D. Individuals endured hardship for Americans to have freedom.
    E. No one individual is above the law.

Answer:

QUESTION 11

Lincoln argued that breaking the law has which consequence?

    A. undermines the nation's values
    B. creates ciaos
    C. prevents bad laws from being repelled
    D. creates division
    E. causes tension between communities and police units

Answer:

QUESTION 12

What is the meaning of the word <u>urge</u> used in the second paragraph of Passage 1?

    A. order
    B. advocates
    C. demand
    D. allow
    E. hasten

Answer:

QUESTION 13

What is the purpose of "When I so pressingly urge a strict observance of all the laws, let me not be understood as saying there are no bad laws, nor that grievances may not arise, for the redress of which, no legal provisions have been made?"

A. corrects a possible misinterpretation
B. provides additional supporting details
C. corrects a mistake
D. provides a balanced viewpoint
E. substantiates a central assumption

Answer:

QUESTION 14

What is the meaning of perchance in the second paragraph of Passage 2?

A. before
B. perhaps
C. therefore
D. certainly
E. inevitable

Answer:

QUESTION 15

Why does Thoreau use questions at the end of the first paragraph in Passage 2?

A. show the importance of the issues
B. questions he needs answers to
C. opens the readers mind to insightful questions
D. questions he will address in his excerpt
E. establishes suspense

Answer:

QUESTION 16

In passage 2, Thoreau write "…life be a counter friction to stop the machine." Machine is referring to

    A. law.

    B. injustice.

    C. government.

    D. spring.

    E. pulley.

Answer:

QUESTION 17

Which of the following best describes the tone in Passage 2?

    A. optimistic

    B. forceful

    C. negative

    D. demeaning

    E. hopeful

Answer:

QUESTION 18

The primary purpose of each passage is to

- A. discuss the options to fight bad laws.
- B. discuss the ways to repel bad laws.
- C. discuss rights and responsibilities of individuals.
- D. discuss which laws are just and unjust and whether to follow those laws.
- E. discuss the idea whether individuals should follow all of the country's law.

Answer:

QUESTION 19

Both passages agree that

- A. laws should always be followed.
- B. all laws are good.
- C. all laws are bad.
- D. not all laws are just.
- E. individuals must decide to follow the law.

Answer:

QUESTION 20

Passage 1 takes more of a _____ approach as oppose to Passage 2 when it comes to unjust laws.

- A. civil
- B. forceful
- C. agreeable
- D. stronger
- E. effective

Answer:

Written by Anonymous Author

In America, jobs are going overseas; in particular, the jobs that require less formal education are going rapidly to overseas countries. Many of the uneducated individuals are upset that they are having difficulty getting jobs. Most of these uneducated people start blaming others for their problems, but they only have themselves to blame. Jobs that required skills and formal education are remaining in the United States. In fact, some skilled jobs remain vacant as there is a shortage of skilled employees. My advice for the uneducated is to get educated. Most of the uneducated individuals likely fooled around in secondary education and were unable to get into college to get a formal education. Others dropped out of college because they fooled around. Also, parents need to do a better job early on communicating the importance of education and keeping their children focused in school. If individuals decided not to take school seriously, then finding a job is going to be difficult, and they should not be surprised and bear full responsibilities. Businesses are going to do what is best for their companies to reduce cost, which includes shipping jobs overseas.

QUESTION 21

What is the main issue discussed in the passage?

A. jobs going overseas
B. uneducated people blaming others for their difficulty in getting jobs
C. parents not doing a good job with keeping children focused in school
D. uneducated people need to stop fooling around
E. college can solve most of the job problems

Answer:

QUESTION 22

Which of the following best describes the tone of the author?

- A. anger
- B. taunting
- C. serious
- D. forceful
- E. reluctant

Answer:

QUESTION 23

Which of the following best describes the person who wrote the passage?

- A. uneducated
- B. educated
- C. a businessman
- D. unemployed
- E. a scientist

Answer:

Written by Jake B.

The history of Russia is replete with sorrow. Rarely did any of its rulers work to better the lives of ordinary citizens. Instead, all occasional attempts at reforms led to more hardships, under any form of government. These changes all too often ended in lost harvests and further dislocation of the desperately poor peasants. The many long wars and revolutions that resulted have taken the lives of many citizens, and the remaining people have to change their lives by arbitrary fiat. Russia has perhaps had more tragedy than triumph. Throughout its long history, Russia has seen dramatic changes in its culture, politic, religion, economy, education, and military. The Russian people have suffered more than their share of repression and misery.

QUESTION 24

Based on the excerpt, it can be inferred that

- A. the people of Russia did not have the power.
- B. the government made efforts to help out.
- C. changes were not happening.
- D. only poor peasants died in the wars.
- E. individuals still had jobs to support families.

Answer:

QUESTION 25

What is the main idea of the excerpt?

- A. Russia has had rulers that have not looked out for ordinary citizens.
- B. Russia has endured a long history of repression and misery.
- C. Russia has seen a lot of changes throughout history.
- D. Russia has perhaps had more tragedy than triumph.
- E. The poor peasants of Russia have suffered the most due to leadership.

Answer:

QUESTION 26

What is the meaning of the word fiat?

- A. foundation
- B. order
- C. request
- D. denial
- E. question

Answer:

Written by Anonymous Author

To comprehend any relationship, one must truly grasp the meaning and understanding of communication along with the various forms of communication. First, communication is the exchange of thoughts, messages, or information, as by speech, signals, writing, or behavior. In order for true communication to be attained, there is both a giving and a taking. If each person participates in the communication, both partaking and being attentive to the other involved, this can be accomplished. As said before, communication comes in many forms such as: verbal, non-verbal, and the media. Letters, diaries, newspapers, books, news, and documents are all forms in which communication can occur. There is another side of communication, which would be referred to as dead silence. The abstinence of communication can portray a message of disgust or abhorrence of another.

QUESTION 27

Which of the following is not a form of communication mentioned in the excerpt?

- A. newspaper
- B. speech
- C. writing
- D. music
- E. gestures

Answer:

QUESTION 28

What is the meaning of the word partaking?

- A. rushing
- B. focused
- C. separate
- D. receiving
- E. contributing

Answer:

QUESTION 29

What is the purpose of the paragraph?

- A. explain the purpose of communicating
- B. understand communication and its forms
- C. understand the verbal forms of communication
- D. explain how communication impacts lives
- E. understand the forms of communication to use with different situations

Answer:

Below is an essay written by David Clarke:

James Buchanan Eads, well-known for his inventiveness and reasoning, is the architect of one of America's greatest infrastructures, the Eads Bridge, located in St. Louis, Missouri. Still in operation today, the Eads Bridge was the first bridge built with a structural...Most astonishing is the fact that it was designed by a self-taught genius who had never constructed a bridge before. Born in Lawrenceburg, Indiana in 1820, Eads received very little early education...His employers saw potential with Eads, and they gave him opportunity to gain knowledge; so began his education as an engineer...Eads saw a problem and came up with a solution...

Eads' interest in rivers had always been inspired by his desire of St. Louis as a major play in an international network of markets. At the end of the Civil War, the dreams of a bridge across the Mississippi River at St. Louis were revamped. Eads saw that a bridge was inevitable by the late 1960s as the width of the river at St. Louis had created a problem with commercial transportation after the advent of the railroads. Because a bridge was not available, cargos had to be off-loaded from trains to ferry boats, which was costly and lengthy process.

Unwilling to give up on St. Louis's future, Eads developed a plan, which was approved in 1867...Immediately, his plans received negative feedback, especially by experience bridge-builders. Reluctant to allow others to dismiss his idea, Eads gave calculations to support his idea.

In completing the bridge, Eads encountered any challenges. One of the most complex parts was not to build the steel superstructure of the bridge but rather to dig the foundations for stone abutments...Adding limestone blocks, the weight ultimately caused the caisson to sink into the river, and within few weeks, the box of the caisson had touched the bottom of the Mississippi River. Airlocks, pressure equalized to what was in caisson, were given for the men who began to work inside the caisson. Soon workers were getting sick due to the expansion of nitrogen in the bloodstream due to high pressure at great depths. Concerned about the health of workers, Eads reduced working hours for all individuals. Still, 15 men died and 76 others suffered severe medical conditions. Other problems included spring floods, forcing men to work tirelessly to stay ahead of rising water. Also, a tornado caused damaged to portions of the superstructure, resulting in months of repair. Eads also had to fight to get the material for the steel...

On July 4th, 1874, the Eads Bridge was officially completed and commissioned. A man with no formal education, enduring all obstacles, triumphed by building a bridge that many said was impossible. Over 100,000 people came to mark the celebration of the masterpiece that was the first important steel structure of any type in the world, resulting in a revolution in construction.

QUESTION 30

What is the main idea expressed in this passage?

A. James Eads success was marked by his construction of the Eads Bridge.
B. James Eads endured many challenges in making his dream of a bridge across the Mississippi River at St. Louis reality.
C. James Eads, an uneducated man, developed a plan to construct one of the most famous bridges in the world.
D. The Eads Bridge was a masterpiece that was the first important steel structure of any type in the world.
E. James Eads encountered many personal and professional difficulties in life, which helped him construct the Eads Bridge.

Answer:

QUESTION 31

The passage demonstrates bias against:

A. architect
B. genius
C. the uneducated
D. businesses
E. construction workers

Answer:

QUESTION 32

This passage uses which of the following organizational patterns?

A. spatial
B. chronological
C. cause-effect
D. problem-solution
E. compare-contrast

Answer:

QUESTION 33

Which of the following is not supported by the passage?

A. Eads dream of a bridge across the Mississippi River at St. Louis surfaced after the Civil War.
B. Eads was a self-taught engineer.
C. Steel structures were non-existence until Eads constructed the Eads Bridge.
D. Eads' early employers supported his desire to become knowledgeable.
E. Eads wanted St. Louis to be a center for commerce.

Answer:

QUESTION 34

Based on the passage, which of the following does NOT characterize Eads?

A. creative
B. genius
C. quick
D. reluctant
E. fighter

Answer:

QUESTION 35

Which of the following is the best title for this passage?

- A. James Eads – The Genius
- B. The Uneducated Genius
- C. Constructing the Impossible Bridge
- D. Triumph over Tragedy
- E. Climbing the Ladder

Answer:

QUESTION 36

What is the meaning of caisson in this passage?

- A. house
- B. structure
- C. foundation
- D. pressure mixture
- E. steel

Answer:

Explanation: Caisson is used to describe a structure in the passage.

QUESTION 37

Today, critics might argue that the Eads Bridge was not a complete success. From the passage, which of the following can support these critics?

- A. Eads was an uneducated man with no real science to back his development.
- B. The cost of the project exceeded what was originally indicated.
- C. Individuals died and suffered medical conditions due to the bridge project.
- D. There were many problems during the construction phase that Eads should have planned for.
- E. The bridge completion was not done on time as originally indicated by the project team.

Answer:

QUESTION 38

The first paragraph and last paragraph mention Eads' lack of formal education. What is the main purpose of taking this approach?

A. to show how education is not always important
B. to show the magnitude of Eads' genius and creativity
C. to inspire others to pursue creative ideas
D. to show the importance of the Eads Bridge
E. to show knowledge can be acquired outside the classroom

Answer:

QUESTION 39

What can be inferred as the most significant lasting impact of the Eads Bridge?

A. established precedent for future bridges
B. increase commerce in the St. Louis area
C. increase tourist to St. Louis
D. revolutionized steel industry
E. showed that formal education is not always needed

Answer:

Writing by Lord Chesterfield

Dear Boy,   Bath, October 4, 1746

    Though I employ so much of my time in writing to you, I confess I have often my doubts whether it is to any purpose. I know how unwelcome advice generally is; I know that those who want it most, like it and follow it least; and I know, too, that the advice of parents, more particularly, is ascribed to the moroseness, the imperiousness, or the garrulity of old age. But then, on the other hand, I flatter myself, that as your own reason, though too young as yet to suggest much to you of itself, is however, strong enough to enable you, both to judge of, and receive plain truths: I flatter myself (I say) that your own reason, young as it is, must tell you, that I can have no interest but yours in the advice I give you; and that consequently, you will at least weigh and consider it well: in which case, some of it will, I hope, have its effect. Do not think that I mean to dictate as a parent; I only mean to advise as a friend, and an indulgent one too: and do not apprehend that I mean to check your pleasures; of which, on the contrary, I only desire to be the guide, not the censor. Let my experience supply your want of it, and clear your way, in the progress of your youth, of those thorns and briars which scratched and disfigured me in the course of mine. I do not, therefore, so much as hint to you, how absolutely dependent you are upon me; that you neither have, nor can have a shilling in the world but from me; and that, as I have no womanish weakness for your person, your merit must, and will, be the only measure of my kindness. I say, I do not hint these things to you, because I am convinced that you will act right, upon more noble and generous principles: I mean, for the sake of doing right, and out of affection and gratitude to me.

    I have so often recommended to you attention and application to whatever you learn, that I do not mention them now as duties; but I point them out to you as conducive, nay, absolutely necessary to your pleasures; for can there be a greater pleasure than to be universally allowed to excel those of one's own age and manner of life? And, consequently, can there be anything more mortifying than to be excelled by them? In this latter case, your shame and regret must be greater than anybody's, because everybody knows the uncommon care which has been taken of your education, and the opportunities you have had of knowing more than others of your age. I do not confine the application which I recommend, singly to the view and emulation of excelling others (though that is a very sensible pleasure and a very warrantable pride); but I mean likewise to excel in the thing itself; for, in my mind, one may as well not know a thing at all, as know it but imperfectly. To know a little of anything, gives neither satisfaction nor credit; but often brings disgrace or ridicule.

QUESTION 40

Which of the following best characterizes how Chesterfield begins his letter?

- A. serious
- B. honest
- C. doubtful
- D. distance
- E. helpful

Answer:

QUESTION 41

"I know, too, that the advice of parents, more particularly, is ascribed to the moroseness, the imperiousness, or the garrulity of old age." This quote shows that Chesterfield understands:

- A. the importance of advice
- B. detachment of youth that comes with age
- C. advice is not always positive
- D. young individuals are not interested in the advice from parents
- E. parents have the right advice

Answer:

QUESTION 42

How does Chesterfield emphasize care without being a doting and bothersome parent?

- A. not being straightforward
- B. writes as a parent
- C. writes as a friend
- D. reflects his past difficulties
- E. writes as a stranger

Answer:

QUESTION 43

Chesterfield uses which of the following when stating "I am convinced that you will act right, upon more noble and generous principles: I mean, for the sake of doing right, and out of affection and gratitude to me."?

- A. emotional appeal
- B. logical appeal
- C. moral appeal
- D. C and B
- E. A and C

Answer:

QUESTION 44

What strategy does Chesterfield use to show the importance of learning?

- A. rhetorical questions
- B. sequencing details
- C. detailed examples
- D. repeating words
- E. using bold words

Answer:

QUESTION 45

Which of the following best describes the tone of the last paragraph?

- A. calm
- B. serious
- C. doubtful
- D. distance
- E. helpful

Answer:

QUESTION 46

What is the meaning of the word garrulity? ~~talkative~~

- A. annoying
- B. talkative
- C. boring
- D. hilarious
- E. unwinding

Answer:

Written by Anonymous Author

The small, quite Amish community in Lancaster County, Pennsylvania, inhabited with about 47,000 residents, never perceived that a formidable tragedy would hit the heart of their community. Unfortunately, on the morning of October 2, 2006, an unspeakable crime was committed. The gunman, Charles Carl Roberts, walked into a small Amish schoolhouse in Nickel Mines and took the lives of five innocent girls. Not only were the residents shocked and stunned by the crime, but the sympathetic nation felt the pain. Consequently, the dreadful school shooting opened the eyes of the public on all walks of life concerning Amish communities across the United States.

QUESTION 47

Which of the following can be inferred from the excerpt?

- A. the tragedy of the shooting opened the doors to further questions of the Amish community
- B. the Amish community was not much open to the general public
- C. the Amish community is not very large ✗
- D. the shooting was one of the most unspeakable crimes committed ✗
- E. the shooting happened because the community is small ✗

Answer:

113

QUESTION 48

From the passage, which of the following is not a synonym of terrifying?

- A. unspeakable
- B. formidable
- C. daunting
- D. tragedy
- E. dreadful

Answer:

Formidable, alarming frightening terrifying, disturbing, fearsome, horrifying

Daunting - intimidating, formidable unsettling, unnerving, dismaying

Passage 1

Today, publishing a book is a difficult endeavor. From writing the content, ensuring no grammar errors, formatting the book, and developing the book cover, getting a book published is a lengthy process. Many writers have good ideas, but are not capable developing book covers or writing without errors. In addition, most difficult is finding a publisher to support the authors as publishers do not want to devote time into a book that might not be lucrative.

Passage 2

Publishing a book can be a daunting task from finding a publisher to developing the book cover. Getting the right publisher is important to ensure the book gets published and distributed, and getting a publisher that provides fair royalties is critical and difficult. However, the notion of online-publishing is becoming a norm in society. Many online companies are emerging that gives potential authors the opportunity to quickly publish work. Some of these companies provide support for formatting and developing book covers. In addition, the process is simple and the royalties are decent, compared to traditional publishers.

QUESTION 49

Which of the following can most strengthen the argument of Passage 2?

- A. Provide data on royalties received from online-publishing vs. traditional publishing.
- B. Examples of work that were completed using online-publishing services.
- C. Name of companies that provide online-publishing services.
- D. Elaborate on how the process is simple.
- E. Delete the first sentence of Passage 2.

Answer:

QUESTION 50

Which of the following is shared in Passage 1 and Passage 2?

    A. publishing can be easy depending on the approach taken
    B. royalties are not easy to get for publishing books
    C. books without errors are more lucrative
    D. book publishing is a difficult task
    E. online-publishing is a norm

Answer:

QUESTION 51

Which of the following best describes the relationship between Passage 1 and Passage 2?

    A. Passage 1 explains the problem and Passage 2 provides examples of the problem.
    B. Passage 1 explains the problem and Passage 2 weakens the position of Passage 1.
    C. Passage 1 explains the problem and Passage 2 provides a possible solution.
    D. Passage 1 explains the problem and Passage 2 elaborates on the problem.
    E. Passage 1 explains the problem and Passage 2 validates the problem.

Answer:

QUESTION 52

Which of the following is the best replacement word for lucrative in the context of Passage 1?

A. good
B. appealing
C. profitable
D. compelling
E. attractive

Answer:

QUESTION 53

Which of the following statements can weaken Passage 1?

A. Writing a successful book is very competitive.
B. There are not many publishers available to select from.
C. Book publishing is not really a hard task; individuals make it hard.
D. Authors can take classes for formatting and developing book covers.
E. Authors can find professionals to support in the development of the book.

Answer:

Written by Thomas Paine, Rights of Man

Every age and generation must be as free to act for itself, *in all cases*, as the ages and generations which preceded it. The vanity and presumption of governing beyond the grave, is the most ridiculous and insolent of all tyrannies.

QUESTION 54

Which of the following can be inferred from the excerpt?

- A. age is not important in life
- B. freedom trumps age
- C. tyranny is ridiculous
- D. laws are critical for organization
- E. all individuals should be free

Answer:

Written by Elizabeth Cady Stanton

Here that great conservator of woman's love, if permitted to assert itself, as it naturally would in freedom against oppression, violence, and war, would hold all these destructive forces in check, for woman knows the cost of life better than man does, and not with her consent would one drop of blood ever be shed, one life sacrificed in vain.

QUESTION 55

Which of the following can undermine the statement?

- A. Example of how women caused destruction.
- B. Success of men in changing society for improvements.
- C. Success of women in changing society for improvements.
- D. Example of how men have done better than women for society.
- E. Example of how men were responsible for America's independence.

Answer:

QUESTION 56

After a test, an instructor asked 5 students in the class how many hours they studied for the test. The students' responses are listed in the table below along with their test scores. Which conclusion is best supported by the table?

Student	Hours Studied	Exam Score
1	15	70
2	20	80
3	3	46
4	1	42
5	30	100

- A. There is no correlation between hours studied and exam scores.
- B. Studying more hours will always get you the perfect score.
- C. Studying more can help in getting better grades.
- D. Studying less will always cause low scores.
- E. None of the above

Answer:

Exam Key – Practice Exam 2

Question Number	Correct Answer	Question Number	Correct Answer
1	B	29	B
2	E	30	B
3	C	31	C
4	B	32	D
5	B	33	A
6	A	34	C
7	D	35	C
8	C	36	B
9	E	37	C
10	B	38	B
11	A	39	B
12	B	40	B
13	A	41	B
14	B	42	C
15	C	43	A
16	C	44	A
17	C	45	B
18	E	46	B
19	D	47	B
20	A	48	C
21	B	49	A
22	A	50	D
23	B	51	C
24	A	52	C
25	B	53	E
26	B	54	E
27	D	55	A
28	E	56	C

NOTE: Getting approximately 80% of the questions correct increases chances of obtaining passing score on the real exam. This varies from different states and university programs.

This page is intentionally left blank.

Reading Practice Exam 2 – Questions and Explanations

Witten by John Down

My dear wife,

I have got a situation in a Factory, in a very pleasant vale about 7 miles from Hudson, and I am to have the whole management of the factory…I was welcome to come to his house at any time; they had on the table pudding, pyes, and fruit of all kind that was in season, and preserves, pickles, vegetables, meat, and everything that a person could wish, and the servants set down at the same table with their masters. They do not think of locking the doors in the country, and you can gather peaches, apples, and all kinds of fruit by the side of the roads. And I can have a barrel of cider holding 32 gallons, for 4s., and they will lend me the barrel till I have emptied it. And I can have 100 lbs. of Beef for 10s… If a man like work he need not want victuals. It is a foolish idea that some people have, that there is too many people come here, it is quite the reverse; there was more than 1000 emigrants came in the day after I landed, and there is four ships have arrived since with emigrants. But there is plenty of room yet, and will for a thousand years to come.

My dear Sukey, all that I want now is to see you, and the dear children here, and then I shall be happy, and not before. You know very well that I should not have left you behind me, if I had money to have took you with me. It was sore against me to do it. But I do not repent of coming, for you know that there was nothing but poverty before me, and to see you and the dear children want was what I could not bear. I would rather cross the Atlantic ten times than hear my children cry for victuals once. Now, my dear, if you can get the Parish to pay for your passage, come directly; for I have not a doubt in my mind I shall be able to keep you in credit. You will find a few inconveniences in crossing the Atlantic, but it will not be long, and when that is over, all is over, for I know that you will like America.

America is not like England, for here no man thinks himself your superior. There is no improper or disgusting equality, for Character has its weight and influence, and the man which is really your superior does not plume himself on being so…There is much attention paid to dress as at any of the watering places in England. Out in the country where I have been you see the young women with their veils and parasols, at the lowest that I saw. Poverty is unknown here…

QUESTION 1

What is the purpose of the letter?

A. to compare England and America
B. to convince his wife to come to America
C. to convince his children to come to America
D. to explain why he can't come back to live with his family
E. to explain how much work he has at his job

Answer: B

Explanation: The main purpose of the letter is to convince his wife to come to America as he misses his wife and children.

QUESTION 2

Which of the following best characterized the tone in the first paragraph?

A. serious
B. colorful
C. appealing
D. desperate
E. personal

Answer: E

Explanation: Down uses a personal tone in the first paragraph with examples of many benefits he receives in order to persuade her to emigrate. He describes details about his personal experiences.

QUESTION 3

In the passage, why does Down concentrate on everyday household items?

A. to show that America has what England has
B. to show that both countries are partially the same
C. to appeal to his wife to emigrate
D. to appeal to his wife desires to be a housewife
E. to show that they can live the same life in England

Answer: C

Explanation: Down focuses on everyday household items since they will hold a special interest to his wife.

QUESTION 4

Why did Down go abroad in the first place?

A. to seek opportunities
B. to provide for his family
C. to explore the world
D. to reunite with his parents
E. to live a better life

Answer: B

Explanation: Down's family financial situation was not good as he stated "for you know that there was nothing but poverty before me." He went abroad only to support his family as he stated "I would rather cross the Atlantic ten times than hear my 45 children cry for victuals once."

QUESTION 5

Which of the following is an assumption indicated in the passage and Down refutes?

A. America is not the same as England.
B. America is getting crowded.
C. America's wealth is limited.
D. America has everything that a family needs.
E. America is a friendly country.

Answer: B

Explanation: Down refutes the assumption that America is getting crowded with the following statement: "It is a foolish idea that some people have, that there is too many people come here, it is quite the reverse; there was more than 1000 emigrants came in the day after I landed, and there is four ships have arrived since with emigrants."

QUESTION 6

Why does Down indicate multiple times that poverty is unknown in America?

A. to show his wife that they can live a life without ever having to worry about being poor
B. to show the magnitude of wealth in America
C. to show that their children will have opportunities
D. to show he lived a poor life prior to coming to America
E. to show how life can change in America

Answer: A

Explanation: Down's family was poor prior to him going to America. He mentions there is no poverty to convince his wife to emigrate and show his wife that they can live a life without ever having to worry about being poor.

QUESTION 7

It can be inferred that Down's wife journey to America might not be possible because?

    A. She has never traveled before.
    B. She has to come with many children.
    C. The trip duration is longer than she has traveled before.
    D. She does not have the money to come to America.
    E. There are many people trying to come to America.

Answer: D

Explanation: Indicated in the letter "Now, my dear, if you can get the Parish to pay for your passage, come directly; for I have not a doubt in my mind I shall be able to keep you in credit." This shows she does not have the money to come to America.

QUESTION 8

What is the meaning of the word plume in the passage?

    A. show
    B. long
    C. pride
    D. like
    E. influence

Answer: C

Explanation: The meaning of the word plume in the context is pride as "the man which is really your superior does not plume [pride] himself on being so."

QUESTION 9

Which of the following is NOT a way Down describes America?

- A. fair
- B. equal
- C. wealthy
- D. spacious
- E. crowded

Answer: E

Explanation: Down does not describe America as crowded. In fact, he describes it as the opposite with the statement "It is a foolish idea that some people have, that there is too many people come here, it is quite the reverse; there was more than 1000 emigrants came in the day after I landed, and there is four ships have arrived since with emigrants. But there is plenty of room yet, and will for a thousand years to come."

Passage 1

Written by Abraham Lincoln

Let every American, every lover of liberty, every well wisher to his posterity, swear by the blood of the Revolution, never to violate in the least particular, the laws of the country; and never to tolerate their violation by others. As the patriots of seventy-six did to the support of the Declaration of Independence, so to the support of the Constitution and Laws, let every American pledge his life, his property, and his sacred honor;—let every man remember that to violate the law, is to trample on the blood of his father, and to tear the character of his own, and his children's liberty. Let reverence for the laws, be breathed by every American mother, to the lisping babe, that prattles on her lap—let it be taught in schools, in seminaries, and in colleges;—let it be written in Primers, spelling books, and in Almanacs;—let it be preached from the pulpit, proclaimed in legislative halls, and enforced in courts of justice. And, in short, let it become the *political religion* of the nation; and let the old and the young, the rich and the poor, the grave and the gay, of all sexes and tongues, and colors and conditions, sacrifice unceasingly upon its altars. . . .

When I so pressingly urge a strict observance of all the laws, let me not be understood as saying there are no bad laws, nor that grievances may not arise, for the redress of which, no legal provisions have been made. I mean to say no such thing. But I do mean to say, that, although bad laws, if they exist, should be repealed as soon as possible, still while they continue in force, for the sake of example, they should be religiously observed. So also in unprovided cases. If such arise, let proper legal provisions be made for them with the least possible delay; but, till then, let them if not too intolerable, be borne with.

There is no grievance that is a fit object of redress by mob law. In any case that arises, as for instance, the promulgation of abolitionism, one of two positions is necessarily true; that is, the thing is right within itself, and therefore deserves the protection of all law and all good citizens; or, it is wrong, and therefore proper to be prohibited by legal enactments; and in neither case, is the interposition of mob law, either necessary, justifiable, or excusable.

Passage 2

Written by Henry David Thoreau

Unjust laws exist; shall we be content to obey them, or shall we endeavor to amend them, and obey them until we have succeeded, or shall we transgress them at once? Men generally, under such a government as this, think that they ought to wait until they have persuaded the majority to alter them. They think that, if they should resist, the remedy would be worse than the evil. But it is the fault of the government itself that the remedy is worse than the evil. It makes it worse. Why is it not more apt to anticipate and provide for reform? Why does it not cherish its wise minority? Why does it cry and resist before it is hurt? . . .

If the injustice is part of the necessary friction of the machine of government, let it go, let it go; perchance it will wear smooth—certainly the machine will wear out. If the injustice has a spring, or a pulley, or a rope, or a crank, exclusively for itself, then perhaps you may consider whether the remedy will not be worse than the evil; but if it is of such a nature that it requires you to be the agent of injustice to another, then, I say, break the law. Let your life be a counter friction to stop the machine. What I have to do is to see, at any rate, that I do not lend myself to the wrong which I condemn.

As for adopting the ways which the State has provided for remedying the evil, I know not of such ways. They take too much time, and a man's life will be gone. I have other affairs to attend to. I came into this world, not chiefly to make this a good place to live in, but to live in it, be it good or bad. A man has not everything to do, but something; and because he cannot do everything, it is not necessary that he should do something wrong. . . .

QUESTION 10

What is the main idea of the first paragraph of Passage 1?

A. Laws are important to the United States of America.
B. Following the law is a necessity for all Americans.
C. Disobeying the law will result in consequences.
D. Individuals endured hardship for Americans to have freedom.
E. No one individual is above the law.

Answer: B

Explanation: The paragraph discusses that following the law is utmost important, and must be followed by fathers, mothers, children regardless of being old or young, rich or poor, grave or gay, etc.

QUESTION 11

Lincoln argued that breaking the law has which consequence?

A. undermines the nation's values
B. creates ciaos
C. prevents bad laws from being repelled
D. creates division
E. causes tension between communities and police units

Answer: A

Explanation: Lincoln states "let every man remember that to violate the law, is to trample on the blood of his father, and to tear the character of his own, and his children's liberty." This indicates that values will be destroyed when laws are broken.

QUESTION 12

What is the meaning of the word urge used in the second paragraph of Passage 1?

- A. order
- B. advocates
- C. demand
- D. allow
- E. hasten

Answer: B

Explanation: Lincoln states, "I so pressingly urge a strict observance of all the laws." The word "urge" most nearly means advocate, because when Lincoln urges people to obey the laws.

QUESTION 13

What is the purpose of "When I so pressingly urge a strict observance of all the laws, let me not be understood as saying there are no bad laws, nor that grievances may not arise, for the redress of which, no legal provisions have been made?"

- A. corrects a possible misinterpretation
- B. provides additional supporting details
- C. corrects a mistake
- D. provides a balanced viewpoint
- E. substantiates a central assumption

Answer: A

Explanation: This is Lincoln making clear what could be a misunderstanding of his position ("let me not be understood") and to correct that possible misunderstanding.

QUESTION 14

What is the meaning of perchance in the second paragraph of Passage 2?

- A. before
- B. perhaps
- C. therefore
- D. certainly
- E. inevitable

Answer: B

Explanation: The word perchance is meaning perhaps (by some chance).

QUESTION 15

Why does Thoreau use questions at the end of the first paragraph in Passage 2?

- A. show the importance of the issues
- B. questions he needs answers to
- C. opens the readers mind to insightful questions
- D. questions he will address in his excerpt
- E. establishes suspense

Answer: C

Explanation: Thoreau is using questions to get readers to ponder on questions that have open responses. This is a way to engage the reader.

QUESTION 16

In passage 2, Thoreau write "…life be a counter friction to stop the machine." Machine is referring to

- A. law.
- B. injustice.
- C. government.
- D. spring.
- E. pulley.

Answer: C

Explanation: The phrase "life be a counter friction to stop the machine" is connected to the phrase "necessary friction of the machine of government."

QUESTION 17

Which of the following best describes the tone in Passage 2?

- A. optimistic
- B. forceful
- C. negative
- D. demeaning
- E. hopeful

Answer: C

Explanation: Passage 2 establishes a negative tone with phrase like "if they should…worse than the evil" and "I say, break the law." Option B is not the answer as the author is not forcing anything on individuals.

QUESTION 18

The primary purpose of each passage is to

- A. discuss the options to fight bad laws.
- B. discuss the ways to repel bad laws.
- C. discuss rights and responsibilities of individuals.
- D. discuss which laws are just and unjust and whether to follow those laws.
- E. discuss the idea whether individuals should follow all of the country's law.

Answer: E

Explanation: Lincoln and Thoreau give opinion regarding the need to follow or not follow all of the country's laws. Lincoln indicates individuals should always regard the laws: "Let every American . . . swear . . . never to violate in the least particular, the laws of the country." Even bad laws, he states, "while they continue in force, for the sake of example, they should be religiously observed." Thoreau has a lesser regard to following the law, arguing at times that some laws should be broken: "but if it is of such a nature that it requires you to be the agent of injustice to another, then, I say, break the law."

QUESTION 19

Both passages agree that

- A. laws should always be followed.
- B. all laws are good.
- C. all laws are bad.
- D. not all laws are just.
- E. individuals must decide to follow the law.

Answer: D

Explanation: Both passages agree that not all laws are just. Option A is not supported by Passage 2. Option B and C are not supported by either passages. Option E is not discussed in the passages.

QUESTION 20

Passage 1 takes more of a _____ approach as oppose to Passage 2 when it comes to unjust laws.

- A. civil
- B. forceful
- C. agreeable
- D. stronger
- E. effective

Answer: A

Explanation: Passage 1 indicates that laws must be followed and necessary processes must be followed to repel bad laws. This is a more civil approach than Passage 2 of breaking the law.

Written by Anonymous Author

In America, jobs are going overseas; in particular, the jobs that require less formal education are going rapidly to overseas countries. Many of the uneducated individuals are upset that they are having difficulty getting jobs. Most of these uneducated people start blaming others for their problems, but they only have themselves to blame. Jobs that required skills and formal education are remaining in the United States. In fact, some skilled jobs remain vacant as there is a shortage of skilled employees. My advice for the uneducated is to get educated. Most of the uneducated individuals likely fooled around in secondary education and were unable to get into college to get a formal education. Others dropped out of college because they fooled around. Also, parents need to do a better job early on communicating the importance of education and keeping their children focused in school. If individuals decided not to take school seriously, then finding a job is going to be difficult, and they should not be surprised and bear full responsibilities. Businesses are going to do what is best for their companies to reduce cost, which includes shipping jobs overseas.

QUESTION 21

What is the main issue discussed in the passage?

- A. jobs going overseas
- B. uneducated people blaming others for their difficulty in getting jobs
- C. parents not doing a good job with keeping children focused in school
- D. uneducated people need to stop fooling around
- E. college can solve most of the job problems

Answer: B

Explanation: The main issue is that uneducated people are blaming others for not finding a job, but they should only blame themselves. Option A is an issue in the passage, but not the main issue.

QUESTION 22

Which of the following best describes the tone of the author?

- A. anger
- B. taunting
- C. serious
- D. forceful
- E. reluctant

Answer: A

Explanation: The author states: "Most of these uneducated people start blaming others for this problem, but only have themselves to blame." The author also states: "My advice is for the uneducated to get educated." These statements and most of the passage suggest the author is angry toward the uneducated population.

QUESTION 23

Which of the following best describes the person who wrote the passage?

- A. uneducated
- B. educated
- C. a businessman
- D. unemployed
- E. a scientist

Answer: B

Explanation: The author is negative toward those individuals who are uneducated blaming others for the problem. This person who wrote the passage has to be an educated individual. The last sentence might suggest the correct answer is Option C, but the overall passage indicates it is an educated individual.

Written by Jake B.

The history of Russia is replete with sorrow. Rarely did any of its rulers work to better the lives of ordinary citizens. Instead, all occasional attempts at reforms led to more hardships, under any form of government. These changes all too often ended in lost harvests and further dislocation of the desperately poor peasants. The many long wars and revolutions that resulted have taken the lives of many citizens, and the remaining people have to change their lives by arbitrary <u>fiat</u>. Russia has perhaps had more tragedy than triumph. Throughout its long history, Russia has seen dramatic changes in its culture, politic, religion, economy, education, and military. The Russian people have suffered more than their share of repression and misery.

QUESTION 24

Based on the excerpt, it can be inferred that

- A. the people of Russia did not have the power.
- B. the government made efforts to help out.
- C. changes were not happening.
- D. only poor peasants died in the wars.
- E. individuals still had jobs to support families.

Answer: A

Explanation: Option B is not indicated in the paragraph. Changes were happening as indicated by the second to last sentence. Nothing suggests that poor peasants were the only people to die in wars. Option E has nothing to do with the paragraph. Because people were suffering and rulers did not work to better the lives of ordinary citizens, it can be inferred that the people of Russia did not have the power.

QUESTION 25

What is the main idea of the excerpt?

    A. Russia has had rulers that have not looked out for ordinary citizens.
    B. Russia has endured a long history of repression and misery.
    C. Russia has seen a lot of changes throughout history.
    D. Russia has perhaps had more tragedy than triumph.
    E. The poor peasants of Russia have suffered the most due to leadership.

Answer: B

Explanation: The paragraph talks about the history of Russia is "replete with sorrow" and "have suffered more than their share of repression and misery."

QUESTION 26

What is the meaning of the word fiat?

    A. foundation
    B. order
    C. request
    D. denial
    E. question

Answer: B

Explanation: The word fiat means order in the context of the sentence. People have to change their lives due to an order (fiat) given by someone.

Written by Anonymous Author

To comprehend any relationship, one must truly grasp the meaning and understanding of communication along with the various forms of communication. First, communication is the exchange of thoughts, messages, or information, as by speech, signals, writing, or behavior. In order for true communication to be attained, there is both a giving and a taking. If each person participates in the communication, both <u>partaking</u> and being attentive to the other involved, this can be accomplished. As said before, communication comes in many forms such as: verbal, non-verbal, and the media. Letters, diaries, newspapers, books, news, and documents are all forms in which communication can occur. There is another side of communication, which would be referred to as dead silence. The abstinence of communication can portray a message of disgust or abhorrence of another.

QUESTION 27

Which of the following is not a form of communication mentioned in the excerpt?

- A. newspaper
- B. speech
- C. writing
- D. music
- E. gestures

Answer: D

Explanation: Music is a form of communication, but it is not mentioned in the excerpt.

QUESTION 28

What is the meaning of the word partaking?

- A. rushing
- B. focused
- C. separate
- D. receiving
- E. contributing

Answer: E

Explanation: In the context of the paragraph, the word partaking means contributing.

QUESTION 29

What is the purpose of the paragraph?

- A. explain the purpose of communicating
- B. understand communication and its forms
- C. understand the verbal forms of communication
- D. explain how communication impacts lives
- E. understand the forms of communication to use with different situations

Answer: B

Explanation: The first sentence clearly states the thesis statement of the paragraph, which is to grasp the meaning and understanding of communication along with the various forms of communication.

Below is an essay written by David Clarke:

James Buchanan Eads, well-known for his inventiveness and reasoning, is the architect of one of America's greatest infrastructures, the Eads Bridge, located in St. Louis, Missouri. Still in operation today, the Eads Bridge was the first bridge built with a structural…Most astonishing is the fact that it was designed by a self-taught genius who had never constructed a bridge before. Born in Lawrenceburg, Indiana in 1820, Eads received very little early education…His employers saw potential with Eads, and they gave him opportunity to gain knowledge; so began his education as an engineer…Eads saw a problem and came up with a solution…

Eads' interest in rivers had always been inspired by his desire of St. Louis as a major play in an international network of markets. At the end of the Civil War, the dreams of a bridge across the Mississippi River at St. Louis were revamped. Eads saw that a bridge was inevitable by the late 1960s as the width of the river at St. Louis had created a problem with commercial transportation after the advent of the railroads. Because a bridge was not available, cargos had to be off-loaded from trains to ferry boats, which was costly and lengthy process.

Unwilling to give up on St. Louis's future, Eads developed a plan, which was approved in 1867…Immediately, his plans received negative feedback, especially by experience bridge-builders. Reluctant to allow others to dismiss his idea, Eads gave calculations to support his idea.

In completing the bridge, Eads encountered any challenges. One of the most complex parts was not to build the steel superstructure of the bridge but rather to dig the foundations for stone abutments…Adding limestone blocks, the weight ultimately caused the caisson to sink into the river, and within few weeks, the box of the caisson had touched the bottom of the Mississippi River. Airlocks, pressure equalized to what was in caisson, were given for the men who began to work inside the caisson. Soon workers were getting sick due to the expansion of nitrogen in the bloodstream due to high pressure at great depths. Concerned about the health of workers, Eads reduced working hours for all individuals. Still, 15 men died and 76 others suffered severe medical conditions. Other problems included spring floods, forcing men to work tirelessly to stay ahead of rising water. Also, a tornado caused damaged to portions of the superstructure, resulting in months of repair. Eads also had to fight to get the material for the steel…

On July 4th, 1874, the Eads Bridge was officially completed and commissioned. A man with no formal education, enduring all obstacles, triumphed by building a bridge that many said was impossible. Over 100,000 people came to mark the celebration of the masterpiece that was the first important steel structure of any type in the world, resulting in a revolution in construction.

QUESTION 30

What is the main idea expressed in this passage?

A. James Eads success was marked by his construction of the Eads Bridge.
B. James Eads endured many challenges in making his dream of a bridge across the Mississippi River at St. Louis reality .
C. James Eads, an uneducated man, developed a plan to construct one of the most famous bridges in the world.
D. The Eads Bridge was a masterpiece that was the first important steel structure of any type in the world.
E. James Eads encountered many personal and professional difficulties in life, which helped him construct the Eads Bridge.

Answer: B

Explanation: Most of the essay discusses the challenges that Eads encountered when building the bridge across the Mississippi River at St. Louis. In addition, the essay discusses how Eads endured each of the challenges he faced. The concluding paragraph summarizes the main idea of the passage with "A man with no formal education in engineering, enduring all obstacles, triumphed…"

QUESTION 31

The passage demonstrates bias against:

A. architect
B. genius
C. the uneducated
D. businesses
E. construction workers

Answer: C

Explanation: When Eads' developed a plan for a bridge across the Mississippi River at St. Louis, many renowned architects quickly criticized Eads' idea. This shows that those that are educated are bias against the uneducated.

QUESTION 32

This passage uses which of the following organizational patterns?

A. spatial
B. chronological
C. cause-effect
D. problem-solution
E. compare-contrast

Answer: D

Explanation: The essay discusses problems Eads encountered along with solutions; this approach is taken multiple times throughout the essay. In fact, in the second paragraph, it states "Eads saw a problem and came up with a solution."

QUESTION 33

Which of the following is not supported by the passage?

A. Eads dream of a bridge across the Mississippi River at St. Louis surfaced after the Civil War.
B. Eads was a self-taught engineer.
C. Steel structures were non-existence until Eads constructed the Eads Bridge.
D. Eads' early employers supported his desire to become knowledgeable.
E. Eads wanted St. Louis to be a center for commerce.

Answer: A

Explanation: The passage states: "At the end of the Civil War, the dreams of a bridge across the Mississippi River at St. Louis were revamped." This indicates that Eads' had the idea for the bridge before the Civil War.

QUESTION 34

Based on the passage, which of the following does NOT characterize Eads?

- A. creative
- B. genius
- C. quick
- D. reluctant
- E. fighter

Answer: C

Explanation: Nothing in the passage suggests that Eads was fast.

QUESTION 35

Which of the following is the best title for this passage?

- A. James Eads – The Genius
- B. The Uneducated Genius
- C. Constructing the Impossible Bridge
- D. Triumph over Tragedy
- E. Climbing the Ladder

Answer: C

Explanation: Option A and B focus more on James Eads, but the passage is more about the Bridge that Eads constructed. The best title for the essay is Option C. Option C focuses on the bridge, which nearly five paragraphs focus on.

QUESTION 36

What is the meaning of caisson in this passage?

- A. house
- B. structure
- C. foundation
- D. pressure mixture
- E. steel

Answer: B

Explanation: Caisson is used to describe a structure in the passage.

QUESTION 37

Today, critics might argue that the Eads Bridge was not a complete success. From the passage, which of the following can support these critics?

- A. Eads was an uneducated man with no real science to back his development.
- B. The cost of the project exceeded what was originally indicated.
- C. Individuals died and suffered medical conditions due to the bridge project.
- D. There were many problems during the construction phase that Eads should have planned for.
- E. The bridge completion was not done on time as originally indicated by the project team.

Answer: C

Explanation: Individuals dying and suffering medical conditions can cause to question the success of any project or activity.

QUESTION 38

The first paragraph and last paragraph mention Eads' lack of formal education. What is the main purpose of taking this approach?

    A. to show how education is not always important
    B. to show the magnitude of Eads' genius and creativity
    C. to inspire others to pursue creative ideas
    D. to show the importance of the Eads Bridge
    E. to show knowledge can be acquired outside the classroom

Answer: B

Explanation: Indicating Eads' lack of formal education with the accomplishment of the Eads Bridge is to show the magnitude of Eads' genius and creativity.

QUESTION 39

What can be inferred as the most significant lasting impact of the Eads Bridge?

    A. established precedent for future bridges
    B. increase commerce in the St. Louis area
    C. increase tourist to St. Louis
    D. revolutionized steel industry
    E. showed that formal education is not always needed

Answer: B

Explanation: The most significant lasting impact of the Eads Bridge is that it increased commerce. The bridge is still used today as indicated in the first paragraph, and the bridge allows increase commercial transportation.

Writing by Lord Chesterfield

Dear Boy,   Bath, October 4, 1746

    Though I employ so much of my time in writing to you, I confess I have often my doubts whether it is to any purpose. I know how unwelcome advice generally is; I know that those who want it most, like it and follow it least; and I know, too, that the advice of parents, more particularly, is ascribed to the moroseness, the imperiousness, or the <u>garrulity</u> of old age. But then, on the other hand, I flatter myself, that as your own reason, though too young as yet to suggest much to you of itself, is however, strong enough to enable you, both to judge of, and receive plain truths: I flatter myself (I say) that your own reason, young as it is, must tell you, that I can have no interest but yours in the advice I give you; and that consequently, you will at least weigh and consider it well: in which case, some of it will, I hope, have its effect. Do not think that I mean to dictate as a parent; I only mean to advise as a friend, and an indulgent one too: and do not apprehend that I mean to check your pleasures; of which, on the contrary, I only desire to be the guide, not the censor. Let my experience supply your want of it, and clear your way, in the progress of your youth, of those thorns and briars which scratched and disfigured me in the course of mine. I do not, therefore, so much as hint to you, how absolutely dependent you are upon me; that you neither have, nor can have a shilling in the world but from me; and that, as I have no womanish weakness for your person, your merit must, and will, be the only measure of my kindness. I say, I do not hint these things to you, because I am convinced that you will act right, upon more noble and generous principles: I mean, for the sake of doing right, and out of affection and gratitude to me.

    I have so often recommended to you attention and application to whatever you learn, that I do not mention them now as duties; but I point them out to you as conducive, nay, absolutely necessary to your pleasures; for can there be a greater pleasure than to be universally allowed to excel those of one's own age and manner of life? And, consequently, can there be anything more mortifying than to be excelled by them? In this latter case, your shame and regret must be greater than anybody's, because everybody knows the uncommon care which has been taken of your education, and the opportunities you have had of knowing more than others of your age. I do not confine the application which I recommend, singly to the view and emulation of excelling others (though that is a very sensible pleasure and a very warrantable pride); but I mean likewise to excel in the thing itself; for, in my mind, one may as well not know a thing at all, as know it but imperfectly. To know a little of anything, gives neither satisfaction nor credit; but often brings disgrace or ridicule.

QUESTION 40

Which of the following best characterizes how Chesterfield begins his letter?

- A. serious
- B. honest
- C. doubtful
- D. distance
- E. helpful

Answer: B

Explanation: Chesterfield begins his letter by being honest with his son: "I know how unwelcome advice generally is," he admits. He sets up a tone of candor that one should expect in a father-son letter.

QUESTION 41

"I know, too, that the advice of parents, more particularly, is ascribed to the moroseness, the imperiousness, or the garrulity of old age." This quote shows that Chesterfield understands:

- A. the importance of advice
- B. detachment of youth that comes with age
- C. advice is not always positive
- D. young individuals are not interested in the advice from parents
- E. parents have the right advice

Answer: B

Explanation: Chesterfield is indicating that the advice of parents is moroseness, imperiousness, and garrulity due to parents aging.

QUESTION 42

How does Chesterfield emphasize care without being a doting and bothersome parent?

- A. not being straightforward
- B. writes as a parent
- C. writes as a friend
- D. reflects his past difficulties
- E. writes as a stranger

Answer: C

Explanation: Chesterfield characterizes himself instead as a "guide," and a "friend." He describes from his own past mistakes to steer his son away from them.

QUESTION 43

Chesterfield uses which of the following when stating "I am convinced that you will act right, upon more noble and generous principles: I mean, for the sake of doing right, and out of affection and gratitude to me."?

- A. emotional appeal
- B. logical appeal
- C. moral appeal
- D. C and B
- E. A and C

Answer: A

Explanation: An emotional appeal attempt to cause the audience to feel certain emotions in order to persuade them. Chesterfield uses emotional appeal, in particular guilt, by pushing "noble and generous principles" on his son by prematurely asserting that he will do the right thing. Chesterfield puts pressure on his son to uphold the image

QUESTION 44

What strategy does Chesterfield use to show the importance of learning?

- A. rhetorical questions
- B. sequencing details
- C. detailed examples
- D. repeating words
- E. using bold words

Answer: A

Explanation: Chesterfield uses rhetorical questions to show importance of learning: "…for can there be a greater pleasure than to be universally allowed to excel those of one's own age and manner of life? And, consequently, can there be anything more mortifying than to be excelled by them?"

QUESTION 45

Which of the following best describes the tone of the last paragraph?

- A. calm
- B. serious
- C. doubtful
- D. distance
- E. helpful

Answer: B

Explanation: Chesterfield changes his tone at the end to one that is more stern and serious.

QUESTION 46

What is the meaning of the word garrulity?

- A. annoying
- B. talkative
- C. boring
- D. hilarious
- E. unwinding

Answer: B

Explanation: The word garrulity means excessive talkativeness, especially on trivial matters.

Written by Anonymous Author

The small, quite Amish community in Lancaster County, Pennsylvania, inhabited with about 47,000 residents, never perceived that a formidable tragedy would hit the heart of their community. Unfortunately, on the morning of October 2, 2006, an unspeakable crime was committed. The gunman, Charles Carl Roberts, walked into a small Amish schoolhouse in Nickel Mines and took the lives of five innocent girls. Not only were the residents shocked and stunned by the crime, but the sympathetic nation felt the pain. Consequently, the dreadful school shooting opened the eyes of the public on all walks of life concerning Amish communities across the United States.

QUESTION 47

Which of the following can be inferred from the excerpt?

A. the tragedy of the shooting opened the doors to further questions of the Amish community
B. the Amish community was not much open to the general public
C. the Amish community is not very large
D. the shooting was one of the most unspeakable crimes committed
E. the shooting happened because the community is small

Answer: B

Explanation: The shooting "opened the eyes of the public on all walks of life," so it can be inferred that the Amish community was not much open to the general public.

QUESTION 48

From the passage, which of the following is not a synonym of terrifying?

- A. unspeakable
- B. formidable
- C. daunting
- D. tragedy
- E. dreadful

Answer: C

Explanation: Formidable, tragedy, unspeakable, and dreadful are synonym of terrifying. Daunting is also a synonym of terrifying, but the word daunting is not used in the excerpt.

Passage 1

Today, publishing a book is a difficult endeavor. From writing the content, ensuring no grammar errors, formatting the book, and developing the book cover, getting a book published is a lengthy process. Many writers have good ideas, but are not capable developing book covers or writing without errors. In addition, most difficult is finding a publisher to support the authors as publishers do not want to devote time into a book that might not be lucrative.

Passage 2

Publishing a book can be a daunting task from finding a publisher to developing the book cover. Getting the right publisher is important to ensure the book gets published and distributed, and getting a publisher that provides fair royalties is critical and difficult. However, the notion of online-publishing is becoming a norm in society. Many online companies are emerging that gives potential authors the opportunity to quickly publish work. Some of these companies provide support for formatting and developing book covers. In addition, the process is simple and the royalties are decent, compared to traditional publishers.

QUESTION 49

Which of the following can most strengthen the argument of Passage 2?

- A. Provide data on royalties received from online-publishing vs. traditional publishing.
- B. Examples of work that were completed using online-publishing services.
- C. Name of companies that provide online-publishing services.
- D. Elaborate on how the process is simple.
- E. Delete the first sentence of Passage 2.

Answer: A

Explanation: Passage 2 states that royalties are decent, so to provide data on how online-publishing royalties are better than traditional publishing will strengthen the argument of Passage 2.

QUESTION 50

Which of the following is shared in Passage 1 and Passage 2?

A. publishing can be easy depending on the approach taken
B. royalties are not easy to get for publishing books
C. books without errors are more lucrative
D. book publishing is a difficult task
E. online-publishing is a norm

Answer: D

Explanation: Both passages state that publishing a book can be difficult. Passage 1 state: "Today, publishing a book has been very difficult endeavor." Passage 2 state: Publishing a book can be daunting tasks from finding a publisher to developing the book cover.

QUESTION 51

Which of the following best describes the relationship between Passage 1 and Passage 2?

A. Passage 1 explains the problem and Passage 2 provides examples of the problem.
B. Passage 1 explains the problem and Passage 2 weakens the position of Passage 1.
C. Passage 1 explains the problem and Passage 2 provides a possible solution.
D. Passage 1 explains the problem and Passage 2 elaborates on the problem.
E. Passage 1 explains the problem and Passage 2 validates the problem.

Answer: C

Explanation: Passage 1 states a problem regarding publishing while Passage 2 states a possible solution of online-publishing.

QUESTION 52

Which of the following is the best replacement word for lucrative in the context of Passage 1?

A. good
B. appealing
C. profitable
D. compelling
E. attractive

Answer: C

Explanation: The passage is indicating that the publishers might not want to devote time as it might not be worth it. The best replacement word is profitable.

QUESTION 53

Which of the following statements can weaken Passage 1?

A. Writing a successful book is very competitive.
B. There are not many publishers available to select from.
C. Book publishing is not really a hard task; individuals make it hard.
D. Authors can take classes for formatting and developing book covers.
E. Authors can find professionals to support in the development of the book.

Answer: E

Explanation: Passage 1 argues that book publishing is a difficult task, so stating that authors can find professionals to support in the development of the book will weaken the argument.

Written by Thomas Paine, Rights of Man

Every age and generation must be as free to act for itself, *in all cases*, as the ages and generations which preceded it. The vanity and presumption of governing beyond the grave, is the most ridiculous and insolent of all tyrannies.

QUESTION 54

Which of the following can be inferred from the excerpt?

- A. age is not important in life
- B. freedom trumps age
- C. tyranny is ridiculous
- D. laws are critical for organization
- E. all individuals should be free

Answer: E

Explanation: The excerpt states that all "age and generation must be as free to act for itself." This is indicating that individuals should be free.

Written by Elizabeth Cady Stanton

Here that great conservator of woman's love, if permitted to assert itself, as it naturally would in freedom against oppression, violence, and war, would hold all these destructive forces in check, for woman knows the cost of life better than man does, and not with her consent would one drop of blood ever be shed, one life sacrificed in vain.

QUESTION 55

Which of the following can undermine the statement?

- A. Example of how women caused destruction.
- B. Success of men in changing society for improvements.
- C. Success of women in changing society for improvements.
- D. Example of how men have done better than women for society.
- E. Example of how men were responsible for America's independence.

Answer: A

Explanation: The statement is claiming that women will do well by not dropping one drop of blood or sacrificing one life in vain. Giving an example of how women caused destruction will weaken the writer's statement.

QUESTION 56

After a test, an instructor asked 5 students in the class how many hours they studied for the test. The students' responses are listed in the table below along with their test scores. Which conclusion is best supported by the table?

Student	Hours Studied	Exam Score
1	15	70
2	20	80
3	3	46
4	1	42
5	30	100

A. There is no correlation between hours studied and exam scores.
B. Studying more hours will always get you the perfect score.
C. Studying more can help in getting better grades.
D. Studying less will always cause low scores.
E. None of the above

Answer: C

Explanation: Option B and D include the word "always," which is not conclusively supported by just the data presented. There is a correlation between hours studied and exam score. Option A is eliminated. The more one studies the better the grades. Option C is correct and supported by the data.

This page is intentionally left blank.

PRAXIS® CORE Reading

Core Academic Skills for Educators: Reading

Made in the USA
Lexington, KY
11 February 2018